AN INTRODUCTION TO BIBLE ARCHAEOLOGY

AN INTRODUCTION TO

BIBLE ARCHAEOLOGY

by

Howard F. Vos

MOODY PRESS

CHICAGO

Former Title: *Beginnings in Bible Archaeology*

All Scripture quotations, except where noted otherwise, are from the King James Version of the Bible.

Library of Congress Cataloging in Publication Data
Vos, Howard Frederic, 1925-
  An introduction to Bible archaeology.

  Rev. ed. of: Beginnings in Bible archaeology.
Rev. ed. 1973.
  Bibliography: p. 113.
  Includes index.
  1. Bible—Antiquities. I. Vos, Howard Frederic,
1925-   . Beginnings in Bible archaeology. II. Title.
BS621.V6 1983   220.9'3   83-17422
ISBN 0-8024-0325-5

1 2 3 4 5 6 7 Printing/EB/Year 87 86 85 84 83

Printed in the United States of America

To the memory of
Elizabeth A. Thompson

Contents

Preface

To deal with the whole field of Bible archaeology in a little book is an impossibility; nor has it been the purpose to do so. Rather, an effort is made to provide an introduction for the Christian who may not be familiar with the field. First of all archaeology is defined. Then the writer deals with questions most frequently asked him as he has spoken on the subject in Sunday schools and churches: Why did ancient cities disappear? What is the nature of Near Eastern lands from a geographical standpoint? How does one go about excavating? How does he date what he finds? The next five chapters give illustrations of some of the major types of contributions which archaeology makes to understanding and confirmation of Scripture. The text of the Bible, Bible stories, kings, cities, and libraries are dealt with at this point. Last, the impact of archaeology in the field of apologetics is noted. While part of the discussion may seem to be merely historical in nature, the reader should keep in mind that archaeological sources have been used to reconstruct the historical pattern. If these few brief chapters create an appetite for more knowledge of the subject, and it is hoped that they will, the reader will find a few helpful books listed at the end of this volume.

Acknowledgments

The author wishes to thank the following publishers for permission to use copyrighted material:

American Schools of Oriental Research, for quotation from *What Mean These Stones?* by Millar Burrows.

Broadman Press, for quotations from *Biblical Backgrounds*, by J. M. Adams.

Harper & Brothers, for quotations from *The Bible and Archaeology*, by Frederic Kenyon.

Johns Hopkins Press and William F. Albright, for quotation from *Archaeology and the Religion of Israel*, by W. F. Albright.

Oxford University Press, for quotation from *Bible and Spade*, by S. L. Caiger.

Fleming H. Revell, for quotation from *The Archaeology of Palestine and the Bible*, by W. F. Albright.

Charles Scribner's Sons, for quotation from *General Introduction to the Old Testament: The Text*, by W. H. Green.

University of Chicago Press, for quotation from *Ancient Records of Assyria and Babylonia*, by D. D. Luckenbill.

William B. Eerdmans, for quotation from *International Standard Bible Encyclopedia*, from the article "Text and Manuscripts of the New Testament," by C. F. Sitterly.

1
Nature and Purpose of Bible Archaeology

To many, an archaeologist is a morbid creature who enjoys poking around ancient ruins to discover dead men's bones, bits of pottery, weapons, or tools. Such an idea is far from the truth. Rather, he is something of a scientist, whether amateur or professional; and he interests himself in a study of dead things only as a means of learning about the *life* of an ancient people.

In saying that an archaeologist is a scientist, we do not mean that his is an *exact science* such as mathematics or chemistry, in which certain postulates, formulae, or relationships are always true. Basically, his method of procedure is scientific. His knowledge is acquired by systematic observation or study, and facts discovered are evaluated and classified into an organized body of information. On the basis of facts assembled, hypotheses are formulated and tested; but normally the tests are conducted at such places as the mounds of the Near East instead of with test tubes in laboratories. Moreover, archaeology is a composite science because it seeks assistance from many other sciences. For example, the chemist is called in to analyze ashes or decayed substances in order to determine the building materials, clothing materials, or diet of an ancient; the physical anthropologist is employed to decide the age and sex of human skeletal remains; and the zoologist is asked to discern from animal bones whether a people has had domesticated sheep, cattle, or horses.

While some think of archaeology as a scientific endeavor, others view it as an adventure—a romance. The lure of buried treasure, the pull of the unknown, and the attraction of discovering one's heritage drive many to shoulder pick and spade.

The word *archaeology* means literally a study of ancient things, but the term has come to be used in a fairly specific sense. Usually it applies to a study of excavated materials belonging to a former era. And in line with the purpose of this book, which is to discuss Bible archaeology, we may define it as an examination of ancient things that have been lost and found again, as those recovered objects relate to the study of Scripture and the portrayal of life in Bible times.

In endeavoring to reconstruct the past of ancient peoples, the archaeologist will seek first to understand their environment. Geographical, geological, and climatic factors will loom large in a consideration of this nature. He will try to answer such questions as, Was their life affected by nearness to great trade routes on land or sea? Was the nation protected by natural barriers, or were they sources of inconvenience or disunity? Were natural resources abundant or scarce, and what kinds were available? What bearing did the climate of the area have upon water supply, clothing, or diet?

Second, the archaeologist must find out about the people themselves—the types of houses they built; the forms of government or social organization they constructed; the religious practices in which they engaged; the tools they used; the art they created; and, by interpretation of material finds, the very outlook on life that they possessed. All are included in a well-rounded discussion of a people of another era.

Archaeology can uncover the past of any nation, and almost all countries have societies devoted to such activity, but we are at the present particularly interested in Near Eastern archaeology and, more specifically, in Near Eastern archaeology as it bears on the Bible. In addition to a number of islands, eleven Near Eastern and Mediterranean lands provide information related to Bible archaeology. A listing should be sufficient here; further discussion is provided in chapter 3. The countries include Mesopotamia (ancient Assyria and Babylonia, modern Iraq), Palestine (both Israel and Jordan), Egypt, Lebanon, Syria, Iran, Cyprus, Asia Minor (modern Turkey), Greece, Malta, and Italy.

Remains excavated in those countries serve two functions. First, they throw a great deal of light on the pages of sacred Scripture. Social, religious, and historical matters are better understood because of Near Eastern discovery. Moreover, many Greek and Hebrew words that were incorrectly or insufficiently understood are now accurately comprehended, and it is possible for translators of the newer versions to do a superior piece of work on a number of difficult passages. Second, archaeology provides an excellent apologetic for the veracity of Scripture. Some critics of the Bible have been silenced or made more cautious by the finds of excavators in the Near East, finds which have caused the dead of Bible times to speak again. And by means of their investigations, some archaeologists have been converted or led to a more conservative position concerning Scripture. For example, when Sir William Ramsay started his explorations in Asia Minor, he doubted the historicity of Acts; but his finds there proved the contrary to be true, and he became an ardent advocate of the trustworthiness of Luke's scholarship. And William Foxwell Albright told in chapter 3 of his *Archaeology of Palestine and the Bible* how Near Eastern studies have contributed to a moderation of biblical higher criticism and how his own excavations and explorations in Palestine helped to confirm Scripture and to alter his radical views of the patriarchal narratives.

2

Why Ancient Cities and Civilizations Disappeared

Often the question is asked, What caused cities and empires of the ancient Near East to disappear? Usually the answer includes a number of naturalistic factors such as earthquakes, invasions, economic upheaval, and drying up of water supply. Although those phenomena are significant, the writer maintains that the basic reason for the passing of ancient peoples and powers surrounding Israel is moral and spiritual, and naturalistic explanations are merely secondary.

Of primary importance is the fact that God chose Israel to be His peculiar people. Moses sings: "For the LORD's portion is his people; Jacob is the lot of his inheritance. He found him in a desert land, and in the waste howling wilderness; he led him about, he instructed him, he kept him as the apple of his eye" (Deuteronomy 32:9-10). Another reference to this truth is found in Deuteronomy 7:6: "For thou art an holy people unto the LORD thy God: the LORD thy God hath chosen thee to be a special people unto himself, above all people that are upon the face of the earth." Because of this election that the Jews enjoyed, their enemies became God's enemies. One of Ezekiel's prophecies demonstrates this truth: "Son of man, because that Tyrus hath said against Jerusalem, Aha, she is broken that was the gates of the people . . . now she is laid waste: Therefore thus saith the Lord GOD; Behold, I am against thee, O Tyrus, and will cause many nations to come up against thee, as the sea causeth his waves to come up" (Ezekiel 26:2-3).

Apparently it became an established principle in all of God's dealings with the Gentiles that they were to be judged in a way commensurate with their action toward Israel. This is evidenced in the account of the attack of Amalek (Exodus 17:8-16) and in the test of Gentile nations at the second coming (Matthew 25:31-46). Further confirmation of this fact appears in Jeremiah 50:17-18: "Israel is a scattered sheep; the lions have driven him away: first the king of Assyria hath devoured him; and last this Nebuchadnezzar king of Babylon hath broken his bones. Therefore thus said the LORD of hosts, the God of Israel; Behold, I will punish the king of Babylon and his land, as I have punished the king of Assyria."

Second, it must be observed that God cannot condone the pride of nations. He is a jealous God and will not allow any other to get glory due Himself. Two passages from Isaiah should suffice at this point. "Wherefore it shall come to pass, that when the Lord hath performed his whole work upon mount Zion and on Jerusalem, I will punish the fruit of the stout heart of the king of Assyria, and the glory of his high looks. For he saith, By the strength of my hand I have done it, and by my wisdom; for I am prudent and I have removed the bounds of the people, and have robbed their treasures, and I have put down the inhabitants like a valiant man" (Isaiah 10:12-13). "The LORD of hosts hath purposed it, to stain the pride of all glory, and to bring into contempt all the honourable of the earth" (Isaiah 23:9).

Moreover, according to the first and second commandments, God cannot allow idolatry to go unpunished. Thus the command to Israel: "When the LORD thy God shall bring thee into the land whither thou goest to possess it, and hath cast out many nations before thee . . . And when the LORD thy God shall deliver them before thee; thou shalt smite them, and utterly destroy them; thou shalt make no covenant with them, nor shew mercy unto them: Neither shalt thou make marriages with them . . . For they will turn away thy son from following me, that they may serve other gods: so will the anger of the LORD be kindled against you, and destroy thee suddenly. But thus shall ye deal with them; ye shall destroy their altars, and break down their images, and cut down their groves, and burn their graven images with fire" (Deuteronomy 7:1-5).

Last, in the counsels of divine justice there seems to be a quota of iniquity allowed to a given nation before it is punished either in a minor way or by obliteration. And it seems that God will deal with a nation when it has reached such a place. In Genesis 15, God discussed with Abraham the Hebrew inheritance of the land of Canaan. In the course of the conversation He said: "But in the fourth generation they [the Israelites] shall come hither again: for the iniquity of the Amorites is not yet full" (v. 16). Hundreds of years later, when the time came to give orders to the people concerning their entrance into the promised land, God said, "But thou shalt utterly destroy them; namely, the Hittites, and the Amorites, the Canaanites" (Deuteronomy 20:17). Apparently the iniquity of the Amorites was full by that time.

One may question that those ancient enemies of Israel were as evil as the Bible claims that they were, but even a superficial glance at Canaanite religion alone ably demonstrates their iniquity. Base sex worship was prevalent, and religious prostitution even commanded; human sacrifice was common; and it was a frequent practice—in an effort to placate their gods—to kill young children and bury them in the foundations of a house or public building at the time of construction. The following verse may indicate this practice: "In his days did Hiel the Bethelite build Jericho: he laid the foundation thereof in Abiram his firstborn, and set up the gates thereof in his youngest son Segub, according to the word of the LORD which he spake by Joshua the son of Nun" (1 Kings 16:34; cf. Joshua 6:26). Continuing archaeological and historical studies relative to those nations further demonstrate the justice of God in His dealings with them.

Though the reason for the destruction of ancient Near Eastern cultures was primarily moral and spiritual, God did use secondary phenomena to accomplish His aims. Sometimes an earthquake would destroy a town; occasionally famine decimated, destroyed, or drove away the population of an area; pestilence sometimes depopulated a city or territory; invasion also took its toll, as did the drying up of water supply. When a community was left uninhabited for any length of time or when warfare wrought destruction, houses were left in ruins. When people returned to rebuild, they simply smoothed over the debris (which was largely mud brick) and constructed a new town. In that way, layers of occupation were created, and the level of a city tended to rise until an artificial mound called a *tell* came into existence. Abandoned tells—evidence of God's heavy hand of judgment and emblems of a bygone civilization—appear in abundance in the Near East, awaiting the efforts of archaeologists to unlock their secrets.

Perhaps the question has arisen by now as to why ancient people continued to build their towns on the same mounds. To begin with, rarely was a whole town destroyed by a catastrophe, and it is commonly easier to rebuild where a group of people happen to be than to strike out for unfamiliar surroundings and circumstances. Second, other choice locations probably would already be occupied. Third, their town location had been chosen in the first place because it was easily defensible and had at least a moderate water supply, and such sites were hard to find. Fourth, often a town drew its life from location on a land, sea, or river trade route. Fifth, a town's prosperity frequently came from dominating a rich agricultural hinterland. For those reasons and others, townsfolk who had suffered a catastrophe normally chose to rebuild where they were instead of looking for greener grass and a more perfect mound at some distant location.

3

The Main Geographical
Features of Bible Lands

Geography is the hook on which the events of history are hung. If one would better understand the affairs of his own day, he should give attention to the geographical factors involved; and if he would gain an intelligent perspective on the life and times of the Bible, he will find it imperative to master the basic facts of Near Eastern geography.

The biblical drama is staged in Mesopotamia, Palestine, Egypt, Lebanon (Phoenicia), Syria, Persia, Cyprus, Asia Minor, Greece, Malta, and Italy. The earliest scenes in Genesis, through the call of Abraham and his leaving Ur of the Chaldees, take place in Mesopotamia. Patriarchal wanderings next throw the spotlight on Palestine.

As the plot thickens, the Hebrews for economic reasons move to Egypt, where they spend 430 years and then escape the country by means of divinely wrought plagues on the Egyptians. After wandering in the Sinai wilderness, the Hebrews conquer parts of Palestine and live there through the periods of the judges and the monarchy. Hebrew kings are extensively involved with Phoenicia and Syria. During the latter part of the monarchy, Mesopotamian forces invade Palestine and carry thousands of Jews captive into Assyria and Babylonia. Later the Medo-Persian Empire takes over Babylon, and scenes depicted in Esther and Nehemiah occur at Shushan (ancient Susa), one of the Persian capitals. As the New Testament opens, Palestine serves as the stage for Christ's earthly ministry, while Syria, Cyprus, Asia Minor, Greece,

Malta, and Italy provide the geographical backdrop for Acts and the epistles.

Having observed the general historico-geographical development, we now turn more specifically to a consideration of each of the Bible lands. Bible history begins in the land of Mesopotamia, a term that literally means "land between the rivers," the rivers in question being the Tigris and Euphrates. It should be pointed out, however, that in process of time the territory on both sides of those rivers came to be included in the designation *Mesopotamia*, forming a region measuring some six hundred miles north and south and about three hundred miles east and west. This area is roughly enclosed by the boundaries of the modern state of Iraq.

The Tigris (meaning "straight" or "arrow") River flows through eastern Mesopotamia, and the Euphrates (meaning "fruitful" or "that which makes fruitful") winds through the western part of the area. The former is almost twelve hundred miles in length, and the latter is approximately seventeen hundred. Both rivers flow southeast into the Persian Gulf, just north of which they join to form a single stream. Both overflow their banks annually, leaving a deposit of rich soil that adds greatly to the fertility of the region. The rivers also act as a source of water for irrigation—a necessary operation because the rainfall of the lowland area is only five to ten inches per year. The highlands and the mountainous sections, however, may receive two to four times that much. In ancient times, when the irrigation system was in good condition, Mesopotamia was a prosperous land; but the picture has been different in recent centuries because the great water supply network has fallen into disrepair and because salinization of the soil has occurred. As the Tigris and Euphrates have flowed down through the mountains and hills of northern Mesopotamia over the millennia, they have eroded away billions of tons of soil. Most of that has been deposited in the annual flooding of the rivers and more gradually on a continuing basis in the marshes, lagoons, and lakes that apparently existed in much of southern Mesopotamia in ancient times. Whether there has actually been a significant advance of the coastline in historic times is at present widely debated.

Mesopotamia was divided into two main sections in Bible times. The northern part was called Assyria, which reached the peak of its political power between about 900 and 612 B.C. The main cities of

Assyria—Nineveh, Ashur, and Nimrud—were all located on the Tigris River. Southern Mesopotamia was called Babylonia, or the Land of Shinar, or Chaldea, or Sumer and Akkad. Babylon, the capital, and such important cities as Uruk, Ur, and Larsa were located on or near the Euphrates. Babylonia had two great periods of empire: the Old Babylonian Period, 1830-1550 B.C., during which Hammurabi was the chief figure; and the Neo-Babylonian Period, 615-539 B.C., when Nebuchadnezzar was the guiding light to empire.

The inhabitants of Mesopotamia were people of the soil. Since much of the land was water-laid and therefore without stone, and since trees were scarce, clay brick (burnt or sun-dried) became the chief building material. Clay served as farmland for growing foodstuffs and products that could be manufactured into clothing. It also furnished material for cooking utensils and dinnerware, as well as tablets for writing.

When Abraham left Ur of the Chaldees, he traveled northwest to Haran, a rich commercial center by virtue of its location on the great caravan routes between Mesopotamia and Syria. After the death of his father, Terah, he resumed the journey to Canaan. On the way he doubtless passed through such Syrian cities as Qarqar, Kadesh, and Damascus.

Abraham next arrived in Palestine, stopping for a time at Shechem and Bethel. Palestine is a small land, the territory to the west of Jordan being slightly smaller than Massachusetts. The traditional north-south boundaries of Dan and Beersheba are only 150 miles apart, and the country varies in width from under 30 miles in the north to about 75 in the south. Even this small territory presents a varied terrain. Along the Mediterranean coast is the nearly sea-level maritime plain, which is divided from north to south into the plains of Acre, Sharon, and Philistia. Next come the foothills, or piedmont, ranging from 500 to 1,000 feet. Behind them rise the mountains of the western range, which have an altitude of 2,000 to 4,000 feet. This area is subdivided, north to south, into Galilee, Samaria, and Judah.

The Jordan Valley is the next longitudinal section of Palestine. Its far northern boundary is Mount Hermon, over 9,000 feet high—the highest point in the Holy Land. A few miles to the south was Lake Huleh—about 4 miles long and 3 miles wide and 220 feet above sea level—until it was drained for farmland by Israeli engineers. Some 20 miles farther south, the Jordan tumbles into the Sea of Galilee, 682 feet below sea level. It is 13 miles long and 7 miles wide, with a maximum depth of about 150 feet. From the Sea of Galilee, the Jordan winds down to the Dead Sea—a distance of about 65 miles, but the river meanders some 200 miles. The Jordan averages 90 to 100 feet in width during most of the year but is considerably wider in flood season. The Dead Sea (50 miles long by 11 miles wide), 1,292 feet below sea level, is the lowest body of water in the world. Its maximum depth is 1,300 feet.

To the east of the Jordan, from north to south, are the highlands of Bashan, Gilead, Moab, and Edom, which rise 2,000-4,000 feet above the Mediterranean. Extending across Palestine from Mount Carmel almost to the southern tip of the Sea of Galilee is the great plain of Esdraelon, or Valley of Jezreel, or Plain of Armageddon, about 24 miles in length, one of the most beautiful and fertile plains in the world. Stretching across Palestine south of the Judean hills is the Negev, about 70 miles across. Although the region is very arid today and sparsely populated, evidence suggests that in ancient times it boasted a considerable population.

Palestine is essentially a landlocked country, having no good natural harbors. Moreover, a large part of the terrain is hilly or mountainous, so the Hebrews became a pastoral and agricultural people.

During Jacob's days, Palestine experienced a severe famine, and the Hebrews moved to Egypt, where food apparently was plentiful. Rarely did Egypt suffer a lack of food because the rich soil was constantly supplemented by new deposits laid by the annual flood of the Nile, and river water was always available for irrigation. It has been said that Egypt *is* the Nile, and how true that is; were it not for the Nile, the country would be a vast desert. Along the Mediterranean, rainfall is about 8 to 12 inches, but at Cairo it approximates only 2 inches per year, and it occurs even less frequently to the south. Since 1902, when the Aswan Dam was completed about 600 miles south of Cairo, flooding has been prevented and the irrigation supply more carefully regulated. The role of the Nile in Egyptian life has become even more significant with the completion of the high dam at Aswan in 1971.

In addition to furnishing water for irrigation, personal needs, and cattle, the Nile indirectly provided clothing for the Egyptians because flax was among the crops raised. Papyrus reeds growing along the river were processed into writing material. Moreover, the river provided a highway for the people; from very early times small boats for travel only, as well as large transport barges, have plied the Nile waters. To demonstrate further that Egypt is the Nile, one should take note of the fact that the verdant area of the country stretches in a narrow line along the river, varying from 2 to 10 miles in width.

At its mouth the Nile formed a delta. This pie-shaped section is about 125 miles north and south and 115 miles at its greatest width. Along the eastern edge of the delta lay the land of Goshen, where the children of Israel lived during their 430-year sojourn in Egypt. Sience it is about 125 miles from the Mediterranean to Cairo, at the southern end of the delta, and about 600 miles from Cairo to the first cataract (rough places, or rapids, where the river cut unevenly through its rocky bed) at Aswan, it may be said that Egypt proper, in ancient times, was something like 725 miles from north to south.

After the Exodus, wilderness wanderings, conquest, and the period of the judges, the Hebrews established a kingdom. During the reigns of David and Solomon and again in the days of Ahab, Phoenicia (Lebanon) figured prominently in Hebrew affairs. At the height of their power, the Phoenicians controlled a strip of coastal plain extending some 200 miles north of Mount Carmel. This plain was nowhere more than 4 miles wide and was subdivided into small pockets of land controlled by such city-states as Tyre and Sidon. The Phoenicians dominated part of the Lebanon Mountains, with their magnificent stands of cedars, and became some of the greatest shipbuilders and traders of antiquity. They furnished timber for the temple and know-how for many of Solomon's other building projects.

During the years of the divided kingdom (Israel and Judah), Syria figured prominently in the affairs of the Hebrews, as it was to do again in New Testament times, when it provided the stage for Paul's conversion at Damascus and the headquarters of the early missionary movement at Antioch.

The boundaries of Syria have fluctuated considerably over the centuries. During the days of David and Solomon, the Hebrew kingdom virtually engulfed Syria. When Assyria was strong, the northern boundary of Syria was pushed southward, and eventually the country was occupied by Assyria. In days of Israelite weakness, Syrian kings were able to push their southern boundary southward. When Seleucid kings ruled from Antioch, they managed, at least temporarily, to control most of the old Persian Empire, including Phoenicia and Palestine. Roman provincial organization also gave Syria a rather large territory.

Topographically, Syria consists of a series of strongly marked zones, as does Palestine to the south. Along the Mediterranean is a coastal plain, never more than a few miles wide, much of which is merely a strip of sand dunes. Overlooking this plain is a mountain range occasionally broken by river gorges and extending south to the Lebanons, with their peaks of about ten thousand feet. Behind this is the valley of the Orontes River, along which stood many great cities of antiquity. Then comes an eastern range, which culminates in the Anti-Lebanons and Mount Hermon in the south. From the Anti-Lebanons flow the Barada and Awaj rivers, which create the Damascus Oasis. Farther east, Syria is desert.

During the captivity of the Jewish nation, a new power came to the fore—Persia. Of course Persia controlled Mesopotamia, Syria, Asia Minor, Palestine, and Egypt when she reached her zenith of power, but the seat of her government lay in the land to the east of Mesopotamia along the eastern shore of the Persian Gulf. Except for the maritime plains bordering the Caspian Sea and Persian Gulf, most of Persia consisted of a great plateau, three to five thousand feet in altitude, which stretched from the Tigris to the Indus. The area was somewhat indefinite but certainly encompassed more than six hundred thousand square miles, approximately three times that of Asia Minor. Though such great cities as Babylon retained their importance under Persian suzerainty, the Persians built or enhanced new centers of power at Susa (biblical Shushan), Persepolis, and Ecbatana in the Iranian highlands. Persia (Iran) is a land singularly lacking in rainfall. Only in the regions south and west of the Caspian Sea and in the Zagros Mountain chain in the southwest is rainfall abundant. Much of the interior of the plateau gets only about two inches per year. There great salt and sand deserts stretch across an area about eight hundred miles long by one to two hundred miles wide.

The curtain falls on the Old Testament narrative with the Persians in charge. When it goes up again, new areas of Cyprus, Asia Minor, Greece, Malta, and Italy come into focus as a result of the missionary activities of the apostle Paul. Paul's home was in Asia Minor, and he spent a good deal of time there on all three of his missionary journeys. The average width of the peninsula is 340 miles, and the total area approximates 200,000 square miles—equal to that of New England, Pennsylvania, Maryland, New York, New Jersey, Delaware, and West Virginia.

A great plateau 3,000 to 5,000 feet high constitutes the interior of Asia Minor. This plateau is surrounded on all sides by mountain ranges. Because it is enclosed, much of the plateau is arid. It supports little plant or animal life and is used for grazing sheep. From the Phrygian Mountains on the west of the central plateau extend mountain spurs that delimit substantial valleys. Through those valleys flow rivers that water this fertile region and helped to give life to important cities such as the great cities of Revelation 2 and 3: Ephesus, Smyrna, Pergamum, Thyatira, Sardis, Philadelphia and Laodicea. In northwestern and southeastern Asia Minor were other fertile regions. The latter territory was known as Cilicia, where stood the proud city of Tarsus, hometown of the apostle Paul. The north central part of the peninsula was Hittite territory, where iron resources permitted the production of formidable weapons and aided empire building.

When Barnabas and Paul sailed from Antioch on their first missionary journey, the first stop was Cyprus. Third largest island of the Mediterranean, Cyprus has an area of 3,572 square miles. It is 138 miles long and 60 miles wide. Cyprus is almost evenly divided between mountain and plain. The Kyrenia Range extends along the northern fringe of the island, and the Troodos Range occupies much of the southern part of Cyprus. In the Troodos were mined the huge quantities of copper and on its slopes stood the timber that brought great wealth to Cyprus in ancient times. The central plain, the Mesaria, is some 60 miles long by 30 miles broad. The granary of the island, this plain also produces substantial quantities of vegetables and fruit.

When Paul heard the call of the man from Macedonia, he passed over from Asia Minor into Greece to carry on an evangelizing ministry there. First-century Greece could not boast the glory of the classic age, but the impact of her culture upon the Mediterranean world was still great, and Greek tutors for Roman children were much sought after. Athens was still the cultural center of the land; Thessalonica was a great administrative and commercial city; Philippi served chiefly as a military outpost; and Corinth lay astride the Isthmus of Corinth (about 4 miles wide) and commanded the east-west commerce that traversed the isthmus rather than taking the longer (by about 200 miles) and more dangerous route around the rocky shores of southern Greece

Greece is composed of two parts—the mainland and the Peloponnesus (the mulberry-leaf shaped body of land south of the Isthmus of Corinth). Mountains compartmentalize the country into small valleys and hinder communication and unification. Moreover, they form so much of the terrain that less than one-fifth of the land area (the size of Maine) is arable. Herodotus observed that "to Hellas, poverty has always been a foster-sister"; so the Greeks learned very early to turn to the sea for wealth, and Greece was great only as long as she maintained an active overseas commerce. In New Testament times Greece was organized politically into two Roman provinces: Macedonia in the north and Achaia in the south.

After Paul's three extensive missionary journeys, he was arrested in Jerusalem following a riot that started over the belief that he had illegally taken a Gentile into the court of the Jews at the temple area. When two years of waiting in a Caesarea jail brought no final disposal of his case, Paul appealed to Caesar (equivalent to the supreme court of the Empire) and was transported to Rome for trial. On the way occurred the famous shipwreck at Malta (Melita, Acts 28:1). Malta is an arid, rocky islet 58 miles south of Sicily and 180 miles north of Cape Bon in Tunisia. A little over 17 miles long, 9 miles wide, and 60 miles in circumference, it is the chief island of the Maltese group, which also includes Gozo and Comino Islands. The island of Malta, with its 95 square miles of land, is of limestone formation with thin but fertile soil. Agriculture is its chief occupation, but uncertain rainfall makes farming a rather risky business. Although its average rainfall is 21 inches per year, its rainfall actually varies from 12 to 27 inches, and periods of drought have extended up to 3 years. There are no rivers or rivulets on the island. Springs flow, but most of the water supply is pumped from strata just above sea level. The traditional place of Paul's landing is 8 miles north of the present capital. Paul stayed there three months until favorable sailing weather (Acts 28:11).

Finally Paul and his guards set sail for Italy and landed at Puteoli, chief port of Rome though it was one hundred fifty miles away. Ostia had not yet become the indispensable port of the capital. Slashing diagonally across the center of the Mediterranean, Italy is strategically located for control of that sea, and Rome is strategically located for controlling the peninsula of Italy. The area of Italy comprises about ninety thousand square miles and divides into two regions, the peninsula and the continental region. The boot-shaped peninsula stretches some seven hundred miles toward Africa and is never more than one hundred twenty-five miles wide.

The Alps extend in an irregular twelve-hundred-mile arc across the north, and the Apennines extend the full length of the peninsula in a bow-shaped range about eight hundred miles long. These four-thousand-foot mountains have passes that permit communications and that thrust out spurs to the west to divide the land into such plains as Etruria, Latium, and Campania. The rivers of Italy (except for the Po) are generally not navigable, and the silt deposits at their mouths create malarial marshes.

Italy's primary source of wealth was always agricultural and pastoral. There were also notable mineral deposits in ancient times, especially copper and iron beds in Etruria and Elba. Marble, limestone, timber, and an abundance of good clay were also available during the early centuries after Christ.

Although some evidence suggests that Paul traveled as far as Spain and France on a fourth missionary journey, Italy is the western limit of the staging of the biblical drama. For all practical purposes, the number of Bible lands must be restricted to eleven (twelve if one counts Israel and Jordan as modern political entities instead of viewing Palestine as a geographical unit).

4

Organizing and Conducting an Excavation

To begin with, one should have a good reason for excavating a mound in the Near East. Proving the validity of some Bible portion is not a primary reason, contrary to the belief of many Christians, though such confirmation often comes as a result of archaeological investigation. Rather, the excavator seeks information. He interests himself in locating a city that is known to have existed but has not yet been identified. He endeavors to resolve the doubts many may have concerning the proposed identification of a site. He tries to unravel the past of a city that has great historical, religious, or cultural significance. Or he searches particularly for the information a mound can divulge relative to a Bible character or event. In line with those or other purposes, he makes his choice of a mound and prepares to begin operations.

Before an expedition can progress very far, it must have adequate financing. Sources of support are varied, as a look at the history of Near Eastern archaeology will attest. Sometimes educational institutions have undertaken excavations. Harvard University worked at Samaria; Bryn Mawr College excavated at Tarsus; and the Oriental Institute of the University of Chicago has been active at a number of sites in the Near East, including such cities as Megiddo in Palestine, Persepolis in Iran, and Jarmo in Iraq, as well as the prodigious epigraphic survey in Egypt. Several archaeological societies also have conducted excavations. The British School of Archaeology worked at Old Testament Jericho; the American Schools of Oriental Research cooperated with a number of other ogranizations and institutions at many spots in Palestine, in addition to carrying on some projects for which it was solely responsible (for example, Ezion-geber); the Palestine Exploration Fund, now longer than 115 years in the field, has also engaged in numerous joint activities and individual projects such as Gezer and Eglon.

Museums, too, are interested in Near Eastern archaeology. The University Museum of Philadelphia excavated at Bethshan and Nippur, the British Museum (along with the University Museum of Philadelphia) at Nineveh and Ur, and the Strasbourg Museum at Ras Shamra.

Occasionally benefactors sponsor an expedition. A case in point is the Lachish excavation, financed by Sir Henry Wellcome, Sir Charles Marston, Sir Robert Mond, and Mr. Harry Donscombe Colt. Individuals are also often responsible, in part or in toto, for financing expeditions credited to schools or societies. For instance, Mr. Jacob Schiff of New York gave large sums toward the Harvard excavation at Samaria.

Sometimes an archaeologist is able to undertake his own excavation, which was true of Professor Joseph P. Free of Wheaton College (Illinois), who headed the Dothan expedition. Sir Arthur Evans excavated at Knossos, Crete, at his own expense for thirty-five years.

In recent years, with the rise of nationalism in the Near East, several governments have established departments of antiquities and launched archaeological projects of their own; particularly notable in this regard are Israel, Egypt, and Iraq.

Several expeditions have been financed by unusual means. For instance, when George Smith of the British Museum found a portion of a flood story in the museum's Nineveh collection in 1872, so much interest was stirred up that the *Daily Telegraph* offered £1,000 to Smith to support him in an expedition to look for the rest of the account. Astonishingly enough, he was successful in finding it on the fifth day of excavation.

After the archaeologist has chosen a mound to excavate and arranged support for his expedition, he makes application for permission to excavate to the government of the land in which he wishes to work. Meanwhile, he has been giving careful attention to the selection of a staff. That problem is not too great if members of a museum or university staff undertake the excavation. Since every archaeological endeavor has its special needs, it is impossible here to cover all the types of personnel that might be chosen. In general, however, the group must include those who are familiar with surveying, photography, excavation technique, pottery, anthropology, and the culture of the area in bygone millennia. Of course, one person might be qualified in more than one of those fields.

When the director of the expedition has secured the permit to work in a given location, he next faces the difficulty of making arrangements with the local inhabitants. Sometimes it is necessary to buy a site outright; occasionally a short-term lease is signed. Often the negotiations take very unreasonable turns. Such is not to be unexpected because a modern cemetery or village may occupy the site to be excavated; or an old family home with surrounding fields, olive groves, or vineyards might be perched atop the tell. Moreover, in former decades more than now, nationals tended to be suspicious of archaeological expeditions, feeling that the group really must be looking for buried treasure; their outlook on life is not always such that they can appreciate antiquarian interests. A case in point occurred at the excavation conducted by Xenia Seminary and the American Schools of Oriental Research at Tell Beit Mirsim in Palestine (1926, 1928, 1930, 1932). On one occasion, Dr. William F. Albright, codirector of the expedition, overheard one of the Arabs remark that as soon as they found the gold they expected to find, the workmen should cut the throats of the directors and take the loot for themselves.[1] Fortunately, no such treasure was found.

Unsettled political and social conditions in lands of the Near East can also cause difficulty. While J. L. Starkey was excavating at Tell ed Duweir in Palestine, conditions were chaotic, and he was murdered by Arabs when he attempted to drive to Jerusalem (January 10, 1938). Another case in point was the experience of the University of Pennsylvania expedition to Nippur, Babylonia, 1888. Near the ruins of Babylon, part of the company became detached from the rest of the group and was set upon by marauders, but they managed to escape. As the party neared their destination, they discovered that the tribes of the surrounding territory were engaged in a struggle for pastureland and

1. C. C. McCown, *Ladder of Progress in Palestine* (New York: Harper, 1943), p. 87.

water rights. The nationals eyed the newcomers with distrust, and there were days when anyone who left the camp carried a revolver. Affairs gradually quieted, however, until the expedition found it necessary to terminate activities for the season because of heat and insects. As preparations were made to leave the area, the Arabs staged a robbery attempt, which was foiled. When the whole expedition was about ready to leave the tell, an Arab secretly set fire to the camp, burning the huts of the workmen to the ground and destroying about half of the horses and a large supply of weapons. During the conflagration, Arabs were able to steal a considerable sum of money. But the antiquities were saved, and the members of the excavation party were able to leave safely. During the summer, a plague killed more than fifteen thousand of the inhabitants of the Nippur region, and the following year the Sultan gave protection to another group from the University of Pennsylvania.[2]

After support for an archaeological undertaking has been arranged, permissions to excavate granted, and a staff selected, the problem of equipment and passage next requires attention. Due to the vast diversity of terrain, availability of supply, and degrees of modernization in Near Eastern countries, it is impossible to speak very specifically on this question.

Clothing depends on the climate and the time of the year when digging is carried on. In the more mountainous areas warm clothing is in order. In the lowlands, cooler attire is welcome, as it usually grows extremely hot, especially in late spring and summer.

Foodstuffs, too, must be selected in accordance with the supply in the area of the site to be excavated. In Israel today, for instance, good food can be purchased. One could probably find enough to eat even in outlying areas of Iraq or Iran, but he might have difficulty maintaining a balanced diet or finding foods to which he was accustomed. Therefore, certain canned and processed foods must be bought before arrival.

Adequate camera supplies, transportation facilities such as a jeep, and tools also demand consideration. Then there are minor items like glue for mending broken pottery and manuals, guides, or other books that the director will probably include in his baggage. Some of the excavator's basic tools include pickaxes, small hand-picks, hoes, trowels (square and pointed), an assortment of brushes, wheelbarrows, buckets

2. H. V. Hilprecht, *Recent Research in Bible Lands* (Philadelphia: Wattles, 1896), pp. 49-54.

(preferably rubber), and a spade or two. Employment of these tools varies with the type of materials unearthed and the degree of preservation in which they are found.

Making plans to excavate will not necessarily follow the order outlined above. For instance, sometimes a university or archaeological society has some funds allocated for excavation and a regular staff capable of doing the work, so a place to excavate might come third on the list. Sometimes it is wise to deal with occupants of an area to be excavated in a tentative way before securing a government permit to excavate. If problems of making arrangements to secure rights from the occupants seem too great to hurdle, it would be unwise to proceed with other phases of the project. And occasionally all arrangements for a season of excavation are made with a degree of faith; funding may come last.

When the expedition arrives at the mound to be excavated, camp must be set up or rented quarters occupied, and workers must be engaged to help with the actual task of excavation. In Jordan, Egypt, Iraq, Turkey, and Lebanon, enough archaeological projects have been under way over the years that it is often possible to hire national workers with experience. In Israel, student teams from foreign or Israeli schools are commonly available. Often American or European students are willing to pay their own way to Israel and support themselves while in the country for the privilege of learning the techniques of archaeology. They may even matriculate at the Hebrew University in Jerusalem or the University of Tel Aviv and earn credit for field work and papers written in connection with it.

The next step is to survey the surface of the tell and lay out sections to be excavated by crews of workmen, now organized under the direction of competent supervisors. Of course, every excavation proceeds according to the peculiarities of the site involved. For instance, if the remains of a building are observable, the work areas become the separate rooms of the building. But normally the practice is to lay out ten-meter squares with a narrow strip of soil as a *balk* between. The balk serves as a walkway and a path on which wheelbarrows may be moved toward the dump. Each square has its own number, and objects found in it will be entered in the record book according to the number of the square and the depth at which they were found. This organization of a site is part of an excavation procedure developed by British archaeologists Sir Mortimer Wheeler and Kathleen Kenyon.

Either before or after the survey is completed, a thorough surface exploration should be conducted. Bits of pottery or other objects on or just under the surface may provide clues to the history of the tell. Sometimes a shaft is cut through several layers in one part of the site to discover the date of the various levels and the number of layers of occupation. Thus a general picture of the history of the site is gained. Such knowledge should be a help as later problems of dating and interpretation arise. It is quite beyond the scope of this brief study to discuss in detail either the methods of survey or excavation technique. Should the reader be interested in such matters, A. H. Detweiler's *Manual of Archaeological Surveying* will give information concerning the former; and Kathleen Kenyon's excellent work *Beginning in Archaeology* will provide a great deal of instruction concerning the latter. The former author was professor of architecture at Cornell University until his death in 1970, and the latter was for many years director of the British School of Archaeology in Jerusalem.

A few general statements may be made, however, about methods of excavation. Historically several procedures have been employed. These include tunneling, trenching, sinking a shaft, and the stratigraphic method.

Tunneling has been largely abandoned now because when one digs into a hillside and extracts objects, he destroys a knowledge of their relationship to their surroundings, and interpretations become impossible. Finds have a value only as museum pieces and contribute practically nothing toward the reconstruction of an ancient civilization. This practice belongs to the unscientific beginnings of archaeology.

Trenching is still employed but not in the promiscuous way of some of the early excavators. For instance, a trench may be cut along the face of a city wall to determine its age and type of construction.

Digging a shaft down into a mound is not to be considered as a method of conducting a complete excavation. It was utilized in the past for hunting artifacts and has been employed more recently in arriving at a general knowledge of the contents of mounds that could not be excavated thoroughly at the time, or in gaining an over-all knowledge of a mound preparatory to more thorough digging, as has already been noted above.

The most common procedure adopted today is the stratigraphic method, in which the tell is stripped layer by layer in an effort to gain a complete knowledge of each level of occupation. In so doing, very careful photographing and recording must be observed. All archaeological work is destructive in that, once torn up, a stratum can never be restored; but stratigraphic excavation is particularly destructive, as well as expensive and time-consuming. Therefore, archaeologists generally prefer the partial stratigraphic method, in which the various layers are investigated, but normally only a segment of each layer is removed.

Before beginning actual digging, the director of an expedition must choose a dump site for the deposit of soil and debris from the tell. This should be a spot that offers little likelihood of covering buried antiquities, otherwise the prodigious task of transferring the dump will have to be undertaken.

A typical day at a dig may begin around 6:00. The supervisors of each surveyed section direct the workmen in their removal of soil, exercising great care that nothing be destroyed through carelessness, and personally taking charge when a fragile or broken object or a skeleton is to be lifted from its resting place. Diligence is exercised, too, in photographing each object *in situ* (in position as uncovered). Pickaxes are used to break up surface soil. Oversized hoes, about three or four times the size of a garden hoe, are used to scrape loosened soil into buckets, which are then emptied into wheelbarrows. Both those who fill buckets and those who empty them must watch carefully for any small objects that may have been unearthed. Pieces of pottery are put in buckets and labeled according to the area and level in which they were found. When smashed or whole jars, skeletons, or other objects begin to appear, small hand picks, ice picks, trowels, and brushes are used to free them. Wheelbarrow operators carry on a constant shuttle service to the dump. Workers will probably stop for lunch around 9:30 and, in an extremely hot season or area, may end the excavation day around 1:00 P.M. and eat the noon meal thereafter. Local conditions dictate whether there is an afternoon work session and whether the work week is five or six days in length.

In any case, the work day of the director and other members of the staff is longer than that of the diggers. Pottery fragments have to be sorted and jars restored; records must be checked; objects found are entered in the record book; and film is developed.

Usually a season of excavation does not last long—perhaps two or three months in the spring or summer. Several reasons for that may be given. The hot summer or rainy months hinder operations; professors at universities and colleges find it necessary to return to other duties; and funds run low.

When the excavation is over, it is time for a representative of the local department of antiquities to pay a visit to the scene of operations. He decides what is to be retained for the national museum and what the expedition may carry home. In most Mediterranean lands today virtually no artifacts may leave the country. But there are cases, especially in Egypt during the High Dam project and at times in Jordan, where an excavator has been permitted to take many of his finds as an encouragement to return. Then comes the task of packing the finds and making the other necessary preparations for the homeward journey.

The archaeologist's work is not finished, however. He has the task of writing up the excavation reports and interpreting and publishing his discoveries. And he is left with the memories of the season's activity—which may be filled with pleasantries as he reflects on significant discoveries and successes or regrets as he observes that little has been accomplished. But there might be another opportunity to dig at his chosen site during the next or a subsequent year, so he occupies himself with plans for resumption of excavation.

5

Dating the Finds

The question of how we know either the date of objects found in the ancient tells or the time period to which the layers of occupation themselves should be assigned often arises.

Even in modern times, establishing a calendar has not always been easy, as reference to any popular guide such as *The World Almanac* will demonstrate. The Gregorian Calendar—that which is now in common use—was adopted only gradually by the various countries of the world after its introduction in 1582. Russia did not approve it until 1918, nor Greece until 1923. Think of the confusion that existed as late as the turn of the century, with so many conflicting calendars. Pinpointing a historical event depended on the country in which one resided. Even New Year's Day has not been uniformly celebrated all over the world in the modern era. England, and therefore the American colonies, did not adopt the January 1 date until 1752. In making the changeover, England also switched to the Gregorian style of reckoning and lost eleven days in the process. Actually, George Washington was born on February 11 instead of February 22; the calendar change occurred in the middle of his life.

If such confusion in chronology exists in modern history, one should not be surprised if dating ancient events becomes complex. Actually, the question of how to determine time periods demands a very technical and involved answer that is impossible to attempt briefly. Some helpful observations can be made, however.

To begin with, it should be noted that abundant chronological reckonings have long been available for the modern period, the Middle Ages, and the Roman, Hellenistic, and Greek eras as far back as the golden age of Athens. Beyond that point, the matter grows more difficult. Fortunately, however, archaeological, historical, and literary investigations have increased our knowledge until we are able to attain a fair degree of accuracy for the history of the whole ancient Near East back to about 3000 B.C. John A. Wilson, eminent Egyptologist, stated that as far as Egyptian chronology is concerned, dates around 500 B.C. may be quite precisely set; a margin of ten to fifteen years of error must be allowed for the period 1000-2000 B.C.; and about seventy-five years of error may be expected in the 2,500-year range.[1] Mesopotamian chronology may be pinpointed with approximately the same degree of definiteness, and the chronology of Asia Minor is constantly being refined. Thus the chronology of Palestine, as the land bridge between those three areas, is now more precisely known.

Christians who believe in some form of verbal inspiration have long considered the Bible itself a good sourcebook of chronology. Many have even sought to establish a chronology of human events all the way back to the creation of Adam simply by adding up the years given for the lives of the ancients. It should be quickly noted, however, that although Bishop Ussher (1581-1655) worked out a 4004 B.C. date for the creation of man, others have suggested widely varying dates on the basis of divergent interpretations of some of the biblical data. Moreover, the Septuagint (Greek version of the Old Testament) differs from the Hebrew text and permits even further differences of opinion. Furthermore, there is good evidence of gaps in early biblical chronology. If such gaps exist, it would be impossible to establish a date for the creation of man on the basis of evidence in Holy Writ.[2]

In suggesting that there may be gaps in the early biblical chronology, we do not mean to intimate that Bible reckonings for later eras are unreliable. Just the opposite is true. For the period of the Hebrew

---

1. John A. Wilson, *The Burden of Egypt* (Chicago: U. of Chicago, 1951), p. vii.
2. Helpful discussions of this question are provided in Gleason Archer's *A Survey of Old Testament Introduction*, rev. ed. (Chicago: Moody, 1974), pp. 195-99; "Genesis," in Merrill Unger's *Introductory Guide to the Old Testament* (Grand Rapids: Zondervan, 1952); "Creation," in J. P. Free's *Archaeology and Bible History*, 8th ed. (Wheaton, Ill.: Scripture Press, 1964); B. B. Warfield's *Studies in Theology* (New York: Oxford, 1932), pp. 253-58; and R. K. Harrison's *Introduction to the Old Testament* (Grand Rapids: Eerdmans, 1969), pp. 147-63.

monarchy, for instance, the Scripture is quite exact. E. R. Thiele, in *The Mysterious Numbers of the Hebrew Kings*,[3] has rendered a very valuable service in this regard. Taken in conjunction with secular evidence, the Bible is an important aid in establishing a chronology of the Near East.

One of the most valuable helps in the field of Egyptian chronology is the work of an Egyptian priest named Manetho, who lived about the middle of the third century B.C. He divided Egyptian history, from about 3000 B.C. to his day, into thirty dynasties of rulers. Although only fragments of his work remain, it can be reconstructed with a good deal of certainty by means of quotations appearing in the writings of historians from the first to the ninth centuries of the Christian era. Although Manetho's history has needed some refinement due to his neglecting to allow for partially contemporaneous dynasties, and although there is some divergence between the quotations of it, it furnishes today the essential outline of Egyptian history.

Manetho's contribution is supplemented by the Palermo Stone (so named because it is housed in the Museum of Palermo, Sicily), which covers most of the first five dynasties; the Turin Canon (in Turin, Italy), which has a list of Egyptian kings from the earliest days to about 1600 B.C.; the Karnak King List; and the Sakkarah King List.

When we come to fixing dates for Mesopotamian history, we are also fortunate in having some excellent sources. Perhaps we should begin with a mention of the work of Claudius Ptolemaeus, Greco-Egyptian geographer of the second century, who made a very accurate list of the kings of Egypt, Persia, and Babylonia back to the middle of the eight century B.C. Fortunately, the Khorsabad King List, published by Dr. Arno Poebel of the University of Chicago in 1942, picks up the chronological thread in the eighth century and carries it all the way back to the late third millennium B.C.[4]

An interesting aid to a determination of Mesopotamian chronology is the Assyrian practice of keeping *eponym* lists. Each year was named after a king or one of his officials, and records were kept of the events of that year. Available tablets provide eponyms for the period 893 to 666 B.C.[5]

---

3. New Revised Edition (Grand Rapids: Zondervan, 1982).
4. G. E. Wright and Floyd V. Filson, *The Westminster Historical Atlas to the Bible*, rev. ed. (Philadelphia: Westminster, 1956), p. 12.
5. George A. Barton, *Archaeology and the Bible*, 7th ed. (Philadelphia: American S. S. Union, 1937), p. 57.

Further checks on Mesopotamian chronology are provided in thousands of dated business documents, references in Babylonian and Assyrian records to international relations with Egypt (and Egyptian dates are rather firm), miscellaneous recovered documents discussing chronological reckonings, and tablets that tie certain dated events to astronomical phenomena. The latter are particularly helpful in checking chronology.

By now the reader may be thinking, *It is all very well to establish dates for the kings and historical events of the ancient Near East, but how does that relate particularly to excavation?* The answer is quite simple. When written materials or artifacts found in an occupational layer of a tell can be dated during the reign of a given king whose dates are already known, the whole layer can be assigned to that specific period of history. After two or three strata of a mound are so dated, it is not difficult to reconstruct the general outline of history for the whole mound.

A good illustration of how this works is furnished by the excavation of Frederick J. Bliss at Tell el-Hesy, Palestine, in 1892. Here he found the remains of eight cities, one above the other. In the third layer from the bottom, a tablet was found which, by synchronism with Egyptian history, dated the stratum to about 1400 B.C.. In the fourth city from the bottom was found a glazed seal like those made in Egypt during the twenty-second dynasty (c. 950-750 B.C.). The top two layers contained pottery of Greek origin dating betwen 550 and 350 B.C. The bottom two strata would date before 1400 B.C. and the other two strata, in which no datable objects were found, belong to the period 750 to 550 B.C. It was possible, then, to reconstruct the history of the entire mound with a fair degree of certainty.[6]

It was on the basis of excavation done at this site that Sir Flinders Petrie was able to develop a pottery chronology for Palestine. Observing that styles of pottery differed in various levels of the mound, he concluded that each period had its own typical pottery, which could be distinguished from that of other periods. Pottery is a valid means of dating because, once fired, most of it is indestructible; styles frequently changed, and when buried in an earthquake or fire, pots were of such little value that they were left undisturbed for future generations to excavate. He concluded that pottery found here in certain dated levels

6. Ibid., pp. 99-100.

would be located in similarly dated levels elsewhere in the country. So, even if specifically datable materials were not found in other tells, pottery could be used as a criterion. Petrie's thesis has been proved true, although some of his calculations have been refined.

This illustration demonstrates that a chronology for the Syro-Palestine region is largely dependent on cultural synchronisms between that area and Mesopotamia and Egypt, since the Syro-Palestine territory has for millennia been an international football, kicked around by one major power and then another.

In modern times another aid to the development of Near Eastern chronology has emerged, something of a by-product of atomic science. Dr. W. F. Libby, of the Institute for Nuclear Studies at the University of Chicago, invented a detector capable of determining age by measuring the amount of radioactive carbon remaining in tested material. This has been dubbed the Carbon 14 Method. It was claimed that this device was capable of determining dates up to 15,000 years ago with a possible 5 percent error. Dr. James R. Arnold, also of the Institute of Nuclear Studies, improved the procedure and produced an "Atomic Clock," supposedly able to set dates as far back as 44,000 years with an error of 37 years.[7] A 37-year degree of uncertainty proved to be extremely optomistic; tests commonly are run with an uncertainty factor of 50 to 200 years or more.

Basic to the Carbon 14 technique of dating are certain assumptions that have been reasonably well established. (1) In living organisms, Carbon 14 and Carbon 12 have a constant proportion. (2) After death, Carbon 12 remains stable, while Carbon 14 (radioactive) disintegrates, when an organism dies it ceases to take in Carbon 14. (3) After an organism dies, Carbon 14 disintegrates at a constant rate and has a half-life of 5,730 years. That is to say, an ounce of it would reduce to a half ounce in 5,730 years. That half ounce would reduce to a quarter ounce in another 5,730 years, and so on until there was too little left to be measured. Age is determined by measuring the proportion of Carbon 14 left in the specimen in relation to Carbon 12. It has now been discovered that there is a long-term variation in atmospheric Carbon 14; this fact creates considerable difficulty in establishing dates by this method.[8]

7. *The Biblical Archaeologist*, May 1954, p. 47. Note also two articles in *Eternity* magazine, February 1952, and W. F. Libby, *Radiocarbon Dating* (Chicago: U. of Chicago, 1955).
8. *Chemical and Engineering News*, 21 February 1983, pp. 27-29.

Back to about 4,000 years ago, dates set by the Carbon 14 method and those set by pottery chronology and inscriptional material substantially agree. Unfortunately, claims that this method can accurately establish dates 15,000 to 40,000 years ago cannot be proved or disproved. The method must be employed with caution and seems most helpful when used in combination with other means of dating.

The subject of Near Eastern chronology has occupied the attention of eminent scholars for many decades, and its ramifications fill many volumes. Most of the discussions are far too technical and detailed even to be mentioned here, but it is hoped that these few comments will demonstrate that an archaeologist can be reasonably sure of the dates he assigns to mounds and artifacts.

In dealing with questions of chronology, one should not confuse the conservative dating patterns of archaeologists with the very early dates claimed for the origin of human skeletal remains (an anthropological question) or the great antiquity claimed for the earth's crust (a geological issue). An archaeologist rarely concerns himself with a date earlier than about 10,000 B.C.

6

Archaeology and the Text of the Bible

It is fashionable for the popular press to print articles that cast a cloud of doubt over the trustworthiness of the Bible. While the facts in these articles may be perfectly true, often they are slanted in such a way as to draw an already skeptical public farther away from the Book of books. For instance, in 1947, a particularly pointed assertion was made to the effect that there were at least 150,000 variations in the existing manuscripts of the New Testament.[1] Actually, such statements are not very new; Dr. B. B. Warfield, the great defender of the doctrine of inspiration and professor at Princeton during the last generation, answered someone who in his day said there were 200,000 places in the New Testament where variant readings occur.[2]

It is not fair to the evangelical reader to leave remarks of this nature unanswered or unexplained; for to explain what is involved is to destroy the effect of the allegation. To begin with, there are not 200,000 or 150,000 places in the New Testament where variant readings exist. Actually, the number is a small fraction of such prodigious figures. Such totals were computed by counting all of the divergent readings of a single word; therefore, if a dozen different readings of a given word occurred in the available manuscripts and versions, all twelve were figured in the total—a very misleading sum.

---

1. *Collier's*, 8 November, 1947, p. 6.
2. C. F. Sitterly, "Text and Manuscripts of the New Testament," *The International Standard Bible Encyclopedia*, ed. James Orr (Grand Rapids: Eerdmans, 1949), p. 2955.

The problem is not solved, however, if we simply reduce one of these six-digit totals, for just a few thousand questionable words or phrases could destroy the message of the entire New Testament. Our discussion turns next to the relative value of the manuscripts utilized in New Testament textual criticism. Here we get a great amount of help. There are two classes of New Testament manuscripts: uncial and minuscule. The former are written in a kind of capital-letter script without ligatures and date from the third to the tenth centuries; they number 250. The latter are written in lower case letters and in a cursive or freehand script; they total 2,646, according to the official listing, and date from the ninth to the fifteenth centuries.[3]

As may well be suspected, the older, or uncial, manuscripts are more highly rated as reliable texts of Scripture, and of this class three are held in particular honor. These are called Aleph, A, and B; or Codex Sinaiticus, Codex Alexandrinus, and Codex Vaticanus. Aleph is called Sinaiticus because it was found by Tischendorf at St. Catherine's Monastery on Mount Sinai. The oft-repeated narrative of his three visits to the monastery in 1844, 1853, and 1859, and his ultimate success in rescuing the priceless document need not be recounted here. Suffice it to say that this oldest complete New Testament (dating about A.D. 350) now safely rests in the British Museum. B, or Vaticanus, is generally rated as the most valuable New Testament manuscript. While it is a few years older than Aleph, it is not quite complete. B has been in the Vatican Library at Rome since the fifteenth century, but only after great difficulty was Tischendorf able to publish it in 1867, and the photographic facsimile was not made until 1889-90. Alexandrinus, or A, is so called because it supposedly originated in Alexandria, Egypt. Presented to Charles I of England in 1627 by the Patriarch of Constantinople, it is now kept in the British Museum. This somewhat incomplete New Testament dates to the first half of the fifth century.

The reader will note that none of these three great uncials was available to the translators of the King James Version, who completed their work in 1611. Instead they used a 1550 Greek Testament produced by the French printer, Robert Estienne, who had available to him very few and somewhat inferior manuscripts.[4] It is remarkable that, with such an impediment, so little of the King James Version can

3. Bruce M. Metzger, *The Text of the New Testament* (Oxford: Clarendon, 1964), p. 32.
4. Sir Frederic Kenyon, *The Bible and Archaeology* (New York: Harper, 1940), p. 289.

be improved as a result of more recent discoveries—a wonderful tribute to the miracle of textual preservation.

While there are more than twenty-six hundred minuscules now
known, most of them are of late date, and few play a very active part
in the establishment of the correct text of the New Testament. *This
should heighten the realization that though many variant readings
occur in New Testament manuscripts, most of them appear in late
manuscripts considered to be of inferior value in determining a true
text and are therefore not important.*

But we are still faced with a number of questionable readings, and
the Christian wants assurance that he can depend on his Bible. A word
from Kenyon is helpful at this point: "In the existence of various
readings, therefore, there is nothing strange or disquieting. On the
contrary, it is satisfactory to find that in spite of all these varieties of
detail the substance of the record remains intact."[5] Kenyon's statement
may be supplemented by the assertion of the great New Testament
authority Dr. F. J. A. Hort, who held that only about one word in a
thousand is under sufficient question to require the efforts of the
textual critic to decide the correct reading.[6] When one realizes that the
Greek text that Westcott and Hort published is some five hundred
pages in length and that the words in major question therefore could be
put on a half page of it, his faith in the reliability of the New Testament is materially strengthened. But he may be helped still further by
the statement of Bentley that "the real text of the sacred writings is
competently exact, nor is one article of faith or moral precept either
perverted or lost, choose as awkwardly as you will, choose the worst
by design, out of the whole lump of readings."[7] Perhaps it would be
well at this point to mention that the questioned readings referred to in
these pages are not necessarily errors but rather problematic passages
requiring the efforts of New Testament scholars to solve the difficulty.

No doubt by now the question could be raised, How do we know
which readings in the manuscripts are most reliable? Whole books
have been written on the subject, and it is not within the purpose of
this volume to consider the matter in detail. A few principles, as
suggested by Sitterly, should suffice: (1) older readings are usually

5. Ibid., p. 300.
6. Sitterly, p. 2955.
7. Ibid., p. 2955.

preferred above later ones because less time has elapsed during which corruption of the text might occur, (2) more difficult readings are often preferable to easier ones because copyists tended to remove difficulties, (3) shorter readings are usually preferable to longer ones because scribes tended to supplement, (4) readings are preferable if they best fit the style of the author, (5) readings are preferred which reflect no doctrinal bias,[8] and (6) readings are preferred that best fit the context.

It is one thing to demonstrate that the New Testament text has been remarkably preserved from the fourth century to the present. It is quite another to deal with the assertion that the gospels, for instance, gradually evolved into their present form during the early centuries of the Christian era and that Christ, who was originally considered to be a human being with a unique God-consciousness, in process of time became deified in the minds of the people by virtue of the increasing stories of His miraculous deeds. There was little objective information to hurl against liberalism of this kind during the last century, when its adherents were particularly numerous.

But thanks to the science of papyrology, which has developed so wonderfully during the last few decades, the picture is now very much changed. For the beginnings of this science we must credit B. P. Grenfell and A. S. Hunt, who excavated at Oxyrhynchus in the Fayum of Egypt from 1896 to 1906 and found literally tons of papyri. Those documents, written on a kind of paper made from the papyrus reed of Egypt, covered a wide variety of topics—ranging from grocery lists and personal letters to copies of Homer and portions of Scripture. A number of languages was also represented, and the materials date to the first several centuries of the Christian era. It was possible to make such a find in Egypt because of the lack of rainfall and the preservative nature of the desert sands. Writings of like nature would have decomposed long ago in other lands.

Since the initial discoveries of Grenfell and Hunt, other biblical and nonbiblical papyri have periodically come to light. At present, the number of papyrus fragments of Scripture stands at about seventy-six.[9] These manuscripts help to confirm the text found in the uncials and to bridge the gap between the original and the uncials.

Papyrology has had a phenomenal impact on biblical study. Since

---

8. Ibid., pp. 2955-56.
9. Metzger, p. 32.

many of the papyri date to the first century, it is possible to establish the nature of the grammar of that period and, on the basis of the argument from historical grammar, to date the composition of New Testament books. Says Millar Burrows, "Even in much later manuscripts, as we have seen, the type of Greek represented by the New Testament is that of the first century. Unless we resort to the wholly improbable hypothesis of a deliberate and remarkably successful use of archaic language, it is evident therefore that the books of the New Testament were written in the first century."[10]

More important than the argument from historical grammar, however, was the publication of a papyrus fragment of the gospel of John (known as the Rylands Fragment) in 1935, dated variously by scholars between A.D. 120 and 140. Kenyon's reaction to this evidence is noteworthy:

> This is at any rate objective evidence, not resting on theological prepossessions, and since it is accepted by all those who have had most experience in dating papyrus hands, it may fairly be regarded as valid. If so, the date of the gospel itself must on all grounds of probability be put back into the first century, in order to allow time for the work to get into circulation; and a date toward the end of that century is what Christian tradition has always assigned to it. With regard to the other books of the New Testament there is not much to say. No one doubts that the synoptic gospels belong to a period perceptibly earlier than the fourth gospel, so that the traditional dates round about the fall of Jerusalem remain approximately the latest possible; and the dating of Luke carries with it that of Acts. For the Pauline epistles the only new evidence is that they were circulating as a collection by the end of the second century, and that this collection included Hebrews, but apparently not the pastoral epistles. The extravagant theories of the Baur-van Manen school have fallen to pieces from their own inherent improbabilities. . . . The interval then between the dates of original composition and the earliest extant evidence becomes so small as to be in fact negligible, and the last foundation for any doubt that the Scriptures have come down to us substantially as they were written has now been removed. Both the *authenticity* and the *general integrity* of the books of the New Testament may be regarded as finally established.[11]

Kenyon's testimony demonstrates clearly that archaeological discovery

10. Millar Burrows, *What Mean These Stones?* (New York: Meridian, 1957), pp. 53-54.
11. Kenyon, p. 288.

has brought us so near to the traditional dates of the writing of the gospels that we are virtually breathing down the necks of the apostles. There was no sufficient lapse of time for legends to grow up around the person of Christ, as has been alleged. We may trust that the gospel writers described Jesus as He was—the miracle-working Son of God.

Parenthetically, the recent tendency of some scholars not in the evangelical tradition is to date New Testament books even earlier than traditional orthodoxy. Albright concluded by 1955 that there was "no longer any solid basis for dating *any* book of the New Testament after about A.D. 80."[12] Robinson has rejected many of his earlier radical views and concluded in 1977 that the New Testament books were written between A.D. 47 and A.D. 70.[13]

But the contribution of the papyri does not stop here. In the last century it was thought that the language of the New Testament was some sort of "biblical," "Hebraic," or "Holy Ghost" Greek. In other words, scholars believed that because a large percentage of the words found in the New Testament did not appear in classical Greek, they must have been coined by New Testament writers for the express purpose of conveying their message. Even in the back of *Thayer's Greek Lexicon*, still used by Greek students of our day, about five hundred fifty of these coined words are listed. As a result of the work of Adolf Deissmann, however, the opinion of the scholarly world has changed. While still a pastor at Marburg, Germany, near the end of the last century, he discovered what several suspected before him: New Testament (Koine) Greek was the language of the people of the Roman world. He discovered this by comparing some of the papyri with New Testament Greek. (Incidentally, it must not be thought that no papyri were found in Egypt before the discoveries of Grenfell and Hunt.) He later came to believe that of the some five thousand words in the New Testament, fewer than fifty were coined by the apostles.[14]

It was not long after Deissmann's epochal discovery, until scholars came to recognize that the grammar of the New Testament was good grammar, if judged by first-century standards rather than those of the

12. William F. Albright, *Recent Discoveries in Bible Lands* (New York: Funk & Wagnalls, 1955), p. 136.
13. John A. T. Robinson, *Can We Trust the New Testament?* (Grand Rapids: Eerdmans, 1977), p. 63.
14. Gustav Adolf Deissman, *Light from the Ancient East* (London: Hodder & Stoughton, 1927), p. 78.

classical period. (Actually, it is just as ridiculous to say that New Testament grammar is poor grammar, judged by classical standards, as it is to say that modern English is inferior, judged by that of the Elizabethan era.) Now New Testament Greek has a better reputation among scholars.

Yet one more way in which the papyri benefit New Testament study is in contributing to an understanding of meanings of words. Some words, whose meanings were not clearly comprehended before, have emerged into the bright sunlight of understanding; others have acquired new life and significance—all because we know from the papyri how the people of the first century used and understood those terms. Those who desire to delve into such matters may consult Deissmann's *Light from the Ancient East*, A. T. Robertson's *Grammar of the Greek New Testament in the Light of Historical Research*, or *The Vocabulary of the Greek New Testament Illustrated from the Papyri and Other Non-Literary Sources* by J. H. Moulton and George Milligan.

By now curiosity probably has been aroused concerning the text of the Old Testament. In this regard, the late William Henry Green of Princeton commented, "The Hebrew manuscripts cannot compare with those of the New Testament either in antiquity or number, but they have been written with greater care and exhibit fewer various readings."[15] Robert Dick Wilson, also of the last generation at Princeton, supplemented Green's assertion: "An examination of the Hebrew manuscripts now in existence shows that in the whole Old Testament there are scarcely any variants supported by more than one manuscript out of 200 to 400, in which each book is found. . . . The Massorites have left to us the variants which they gathered and we find that they amount altogether to about 1,200, less than one for each page of the printed Hebrew Bible."[16] Moreover, "The various readings are for the most part of a trivial character, not materially affecting the sense."[17]

Until recent decades, the oldest Hebrew manuscript of any length did not date earlier than the end of the ninth century, and the oldest complete Hebrew Bible dates about a century later. Then, in the

15. William Henry Green, *General Introduction to the Old Testament: The Text* (New York: Scribner, 1898), p. 179.
16. R. D. Wilson, *Scientific Investigation of the Old Testament* (Chicago: Moody, 1959), pp. 69-70.
17. Green, p. 179.

spring of 1948, the religious and academic worlds were rocked with the announcement that an ancient Isaiah manuscript had been found in a cave at the northwest corner of the Dead Sea. Since then a total of eleven caves around Qumran have disgorged their treasures of scrolls or fragments. In addition, portions of biblical scrolls have been found in other caves in the region of the Dead Sea and in excavations at Masada. Tens of thousands of fragments have been recovered. While most of the materials are nonbiblical, several hundred fragments bear Scripture portions. So far, all Old Testament books except Esther are represented in the finds. As might be expected, fragments of Old Testament books quoted most in the New Testament (Deuteronomy, Isaiah, Psalms) are most numerous. The longest and most intact biblical scrolls include two of Isaiah, one of Psalms, and one of Leviticus.

The significance of the Dead Sea Scrolls is tremendous. They have pushed the history of the Old Testament text back 1,000 years (they date during the first two centuries B.C. and the first century A.D.). Second, they have provided an abundance of critical material for research on the Old Testament, comparable to what has been available to New Testament scholars for many years. Third, the Dead Sea Scrolls have provided a more adequate context for the New Testament, demonstrating, for instance, the essential Jewish background of the gospel of John—rather than a Greek background, as scholars have frequently asserted. Fourth, they help to establish the accuracy of the Old Testament text. The Septuagint (Greek Old Testament) has been shown by studies in the scrolls to be more nearly accurate than had previously been thought. Fifth it has been demonstrated that there were other families of texts besides the Masoretic (traditional), which has served as the text of our Hebrew Bibles for so long. Yet, when all of the evidence is in, perhaps scholars will conclude that the true text of the Old Testament is in excess of 95 percent of what we have had in the Masoretic text all along. In this connection, it is interesting to note that the Isaiah manuscript tallies almost exactly with the Masoretic text. Gleason Archer observes that the traditional text of Isaiah is word for word identical with the two long Isaiah scrolls from Cave 1, in 95 percent of the text. The other five percent of variation consists mostly of "obvious slips of the pen and variations in spelling."[18]

---

18. Gleason Archer, *A Survey of Old Testament Introduction*, rev. ed. (Chicago: Moody, 1974), p. 25.

It should be apparent to the reverent Bible student that he need have no fear of so-called scholarly attacks on Scripture. We are now in possession of enough facts to demonstrate that the Bible we love is essentially the message revealed to holy writers of old. We may conclude with Kenyon that "the Christian can take the whole Bible in his hand and say without fear or hesitation that he holds in it the true word of God, handed down without essential loss from generation to generation throughout the centuries."[19]

---

19. Sir Frederic Kenyon, *Our Bible and the Ancient Manuscripts,* 5th ed. (New York: Harper, 1958), p. 55.

7

Archaeology and Bible Narratives

Events in history can hardly be divorced from people; and since many of the individuals connected with Bible narratives were kings, it is difficult to discuss certain happenings of Bible times without involving some of the kings. There is, therefore, quite an affinity between the subject matter of this and the following chapter. For purposes of organization, however, and in an effort to represent the whole field of Bible archaeology, a separate chapter is devoted to these incidents.

The Exodus from Egypt

A biblical event that has captured the imagination of most Christians is the Exodus. In early Sunday school days the child hears stories about the baby Moses in the bulrushes and his later leadership of the Hebrews from Egyptian bondage to the gates of the promised land. Later in life he may ask such questions as, When did this event take place? What Pharaoh ruled at the time? Is there any indication from secular sources as to what the Egyptians thought about all this?

Unfortunately for us, the Egyptians never preserved in their inscriptions anything uncomplimentary to themselves; therefore we gain no help from such sources as to when the Exodus occurred or even whether or not there was such an event. So, when seeking to solve problems of this nature, we must turn to other avenues of information.

It is always a good idea to begin with scriptural evidence. As far as the date of the Exodus is concerned, direct assistance is afforded in 1 Kings 6:1, which asserts that the Exodus took place 480 years before the fourth year of Solomon's reign, when he began the temple. If we base our computation on Thiele's chronology (he assigns 931 B.C. as the date of the end of Solomon's reign and the division of the monarchy),[1] we find that the fourth year of Solomon's forty-year reign was 967 B.C., and the Exodus therefore took place in 1447 B.C. Albright, on the other hand, pegs the schism at 922 B.C.[2] On this basis we arrive at 1438 B.C. for the date of the Exodus. Other chronologies could be suggested, but those two are sufficient to show that 1 Kings 6:1 leads to an approximate date of 1440 B.C. for the Exodus.

Support for this date was provided by the excavations of John Garstang at Jericho (1930-1936). He reported that the Canaanite city fell about 1400 B.C.;[3] and when allowance is made for a forty-year wandering in the wilderness, the date of the Exodus approximates 1440 B.C. In spite of opposition to his conclusions, Garstang reiterated his earlier contention in a postwar work produced in collaboration with his son.[4]

Furthermore, an approximate date of 1400 B.C. for the conquest of Palestine is not impossible from the standpoint of Egyptian history; about that time the Amarna Age began, and Egyptian control in Canaan rapidly disintegrated. The Amarna Period (about 1400-1365 B.C.) was a time when the kings of Egypt were much more interested in making religious reforms and expending the energies of the nation on gratifying their personal desires than they were on maintaining a powerful empire. The royal correspondence found at Amarna demonstrates that Egyptian puppet rulers of Palestine sent the pharaohs frequent calls for help during that half century. Local disturbances and the invasion of the Habiru (possibly related in some way to the Hebrews) were the occasions of such requests. But cushioned amid luxuries of Egypt, the pharaohs chose the path of personal enjoyment rather than royal responsibility. The pleas went unheeded.

---

1. E. R. Thiele, *The Mysterious Numbers of the Hebrew Kings,* new rev. ed. (Grand Rapids: Zondervan, 1982), p. 55.
2. *Bulletin of the American Schools of Oriental Research,* December, 1945, p. 20.
3. John Garstang, *Joshua and Judges* (New York: Harper, 1931), p. 147.
4. John Garstang and J. B. E. Garstang, *The Story of Jericho* (London: Marshall, Morgan & Scott, 1948), p. xiv.

If one turns to the Septuagint version of 1 Kings 6:1, he arrives at a slightly different date for the Exodus. The Septuagint says that the Exodus took place 440 years before the fourth year of Solomon's reign, or about 1400 B.C. That would date the conquest about 1350 B.C. In interesting support of that view, Kathleen Kenyon, in her excavations at Jericho, concluded that the city fell to Joshua somewhere between 1350 and 1325 B.C.[5]

The early date of the Exodus is objected to by such scholars as Albright, who pointed out that Glueck's explorations in Edomite territory revealed that this area had no sedentary population until the thirteenth century B.C.[6] Therefore, the Israelites could not have been stopped by them on their way to Palestine at the beginning of the fourteenth century B.C. However, we may suggest with Unger[7] that as nomads the Edomites could have stopped the Israelites; certainly if the nomadic Israelites were able to carry on warfare, the Edomites likewise could have done so. Or, we could conjecture with Free that Glueck's assignment of dates may need refinement.[8] It should be pointed out that Glueck's conclusions are based on dates assigned to pottery fragments, and Albright himself stated that pottery evidence for dating some of the copper mines west and south of Edom was not conclusive.[9] In recent years aspects of Glueck's chronology for this region have been greatly modified. In fact, Benno Rothenberg concluded that his excavations in the Timna Valley (c. 15 miles north of the Gulf of Aqaba) between 1964 and 1970 would require "reconsideration" of the thirteenth-century date of the Exodus.[10]

Another major problem confronting one who accepts the early date of the Exodus is the fact that the Israelites built Pithom and Raamses (Exodus 1:11). Raamses I did not rule until about 1300 B.C. Unger suggested the difficulty here may be removed by concluding that *Raamses* is a modernization of the ancient place-name *Zoan-Avaris*. A

5. Kathleen Kenyon, *Digging Up Jericho*, (New York: Praeger, 1957), p. 262.
6. William F. Albright, *From the Stone Age to Christianity*, 2d ed. (Baltimore: Johns Hopkins, 1957), p. 195.
7. Merrill F. Unger, *Archaeology and the Old Testament* (Grand Rapids: Zondervan, 1954), p. 151.
8. Joseph P. Free, *Archaeology and Bible History* (Wheaton, Ill.: Scripture Press, 1964), p. 99.
9. Albright, p. 195.
10. Benno Rothenberg, *Were These King Solomon's Mines?* (New York: Stein & Day, 1972), p. 184.

similar situation occurs in Genesis 14:14, where *Dan* is substituted for the older city name of *Laish*.[11]

It should be pointed out that nothing is solved by asserting, as many do, that the Exodus could not have taken place until after 1300 B.C. because the store city of Raamses was named after the ruling pharaoh. Moses was eighty at the time of the Exodus (Exodus 7:7). If the date of the Exodus is set at about 1275, Moses would have been born about 1355. The Hebrews built the store city of Raamses before the birth of Moses, long before the reign of the first Raamses. The town of Raamses may not have been named after the ruling king at all; possibly *Raamses* was a venerated royal or religious name of centuries' standing.

Third, Yigael Yadin, eminent excavator of Hazor, claims that Hazor did not fall to the Israelites until the second third of the thirteenth century B.C.[12] But Scripture indicates that Hazor fell to the Israelites twice: in the days of Joshua (Joshua 11:10-11), when Jabin I ruled; and in the days of Deborah and Barak (Judges 4:2, 23-24), when another Jabin ruled. Yadin assumed that Joshua's conquest is to be related to thirteenth-century destruction in the lower city of Hazor. There was, however, evidence of destruction at the site around 1400 B.C. or a little later in Areas H and K of the lower city.[13] What is more natural than to conclude that the 1400 B.C. destruction dates to Joshua's day and the thirteenth-century destruction dates to the period of the judges?

Fourth, it is argued that the palace's accessibility to Moses militates against the early date of the Exodus. The reasoning is that such accessibility indicates the palace was in the delta region, where the Israelites lived, and the periods when the palace was located in the delta were the days of Joseph and during the thirteenth century B.C. It may be pointed out, however, that the pharaoh of the Exodus could have met Moses at a secondary palace or administrative center. The argument is not conclusive proof for the late date of the Exodus. Moreover, both Thutmose III and Amenhotep II, who ruled 1482-1425, were active in building projects in the delta.

Last, the destruction of Bethel, Lachish, and Debir, presumably by

---

11. Unger, p. 149.
12. Yigael Yadin, "Hazor," in *Encyclopedia of Archaeological Excavations in the Holy Land*, vol. 2, edited by Michael Avi-Yonah (Englewood Cliffs, N.J.: Prentice-Hall, 1976), p. 494.
13. Ibid., pp. 481-2.

Israelites, is claimed to have occurred about 1230 B.C.[14] and therefore to support a late date for the Exodus. Seemingly, this is strong evidence for the late date of the Exodus, but a second glance puts the matter in a different light. Those cities fell about the same time and near the beginning of the conquest, according to the Joshua narrative. But certainly the conquest did not occur as late as 1230 B.C., because the inscription on the Stele of Pharaoh Merneptah represents the Hebrews as settled in Canaan when Merneptah's armies attacked them about 1230 B.C. If adjustment in the dates assigned to the destruction of those sites needs to be made, how effective is the use of the evidence in establishing the date of the Exodus? Additionally, it is important to note that while Joshua captured Bethel, Lachish, and Debir, nothing is said about destroying them; he burned only Ai, Jericho, and Hazor (Joshua 6:24; 8:19; 11:13). Some of Joshua's conquests were not permanent. We know that Debir had to be recaptured later (Joshua 15:13-17), and possibly the others did also. If dates of destruction at Bethel, Lachish, and Debir are correct, they may well refer to attacks during the days of the judges instead of to Joshua's conquests.

On the basis of this discussion, it is clear that we cannot be dogmatic about the date of the Exodus. There are problems facing the one who chooses either the early or late date. But there are answers to all points of opposition to the early date, and the case for it continues to grow stronger. Furthermore, one who holds to a high view of Scripture will not lightly dismiss the indication of 1 Kings 6:1.

It still remains, however, to identify the pharaoh of the oppression and Exodus. If we follow the Steindorff and Seele chronology of Egyptian history,[15] the early date of the Exodus would fall within the reign of Amenhotep II (1450-1425 B.C.), while the pharaoh of the great oppression would be Thutmose III (1482-1450 B.C.). Moreover, since Moses was eighty years old at the time of the Exodus, his birth probably took place during the reign of Thutmose I (1525-1508 B.C.), and his famous daughter was Hatshepsut, possibly the princess who rescued Moses from the reeds along the Nile.

---

14. J. L. Kelso, "Bethel," in *Encyclopedia of Archaeological Excavations in the Holy Land*, vol. 1, edited by Michael Avi-Yonah, p. 192; Y. Aharoni, "Lachish," in ibid., vol. 3, edited by Michael Avi-Yonah and Ephraim Stern, p. 743; W. F. Albright, "Tell Beit Mirsim," in ibid., vol. 1, p. 177.

15. George Steindorff and Keith Seele, *When Egypt Ruled the East* (Chicago: U. of Chicago, 1957), p. 274.

In further interesting relationship to the whole narrative is the Dream Inscription of Thutmose IV (1425-1412 B.C.), the successor of Amenhotep II. As the story goes, one day Prince Thutmose was hunting in the desert and fell asleep in the shadow of the Sphinx, which appeared to him in a dream and told him that he was to be the next king and asked him to rehabilitate the Sphinx. Since Thutmose was so surprised at the announcement, he apparently was not the next in line for the throne and therefore not the oldest son. It may be, then, that his elder brother was killed in the tenth plague.[16] This is not just a story; Thutmose's red granite slab commemorating this dream still stands between the paws of the Sphinx, and any traveler to Egypt may see it there.

In following the date of the fall of Jericho espoused by Miss Kenyon, one might conclude that the Exodus took place during the first half of the fourteenth century. Accordingly, Amenhotep III or IV might have been pharaoh at the time. Those who hold the late date generally conclude that Raamses II (1299-1232 B.C.) was pharaoh of the Exodus.

Hebrew Conquest of Jerusalem

When the Hebrew host, with Commander-in-chief Joshua, invaded the land of Canaan, they were not successful in taking Jerusalem. In fact, it was not until after the forty-year reign of Saul and the seven-year rule of David at Hebron that the mighty warrior of Israel succeeded in making it the capital of the commonwealth. The conquest is described briefly in 2 Samuel 5:6-9 and 1 Chronicles 11:4-8.

From these verses, the general situation is clear. The Jebusites felt secure behind virtually impregnable fortifications—so much so that they said the blind and lame could ward off the attacks of David. The Hebrew king was determined, however, and offered the captaincy of the armed forces to the one who would lead a successful attack against the Jebusite defenders. Joab earned the reward promised by David.

A problem arises, however, in interpreting the method Joab used to accomplish this military feat. Second Samuel 5:8 speaks of ascending the "gutter" in the King James Version, the "watercourse" in the *American Standard Version*, and the "water shaft" in the *Revised*

---

16. S. L. Caiger, *Bible and Spade* (New York: Oxford U., 1951), p. 74.

Standard Version. In recent years, the general opinion has been that the city water supply channel was in view here and that the "watercourse" was to be identified with a discovery of Sir Charles Warren at Jerusalem. He found that since there was no natural water supply within the walls of the ancient city, a water channel had been cut leading from a point inside the walls to the Spring Gihon, or the Virgin's Fountain, on the outside. More specifically, a horizontal tunnel leading from the spring had been dug into the hill on which the city was located; this ended in a cave that served as a cistern. Above the cave rose a 52-foot vertical shaft, which connected with a sloping passageway 127 feet long. The entrance to this passageway was inside the city wall. Women could then descend the sloping passage to the vertical shaft and lower their waterskins into the cave to procure a water supply, in spite of military forces that might be encamped outside the walls. Joab supposedly discovered this water system, ascended the passageway, and entered the city at night, delivering it into the hands of David.

J. Garrow Duncan takes issue with this suggestion, asserting that it is almost humanly impossible to scale the shaft, which is very steep. Furthermore, the sides of it have been worn almost smooth by the constant rubbing of waterskins, to say nothing of the fact that it is so narrow at one point that a large man could not even get through.[17] A. Rendle Short claims, however, that some British army officers were able to accomplish this feat in 1910.[18] The water system was finally cleared in 1980, and two young Americans subsequently did manage to ascend the shaft. The writer met one of them in Jerusalem in 1982.

Duncan also argued that Warren's Shaft led into the lower part of the Jebusite city only, and thus still would not have given David access to the fortress area. In reporting his excavations at Jerusalem, he claimed that part of the eastern wall of the lower city was battered in during Davidic times and that David therefore forced his way into the lower city.[19]

Duncan, puzzled with the meaning of *tsinnor,* translated "watercourse" in the ASV, pointed out that in Aramaic and Arabic, its

---

17. J. Garrow Duncan, *The Accuracy of the Old Testament* (London: S.P.C.K., 1930), pp. 136-38.
18. A. Rendle Short, *Modern Discovery and the Bible,* 3d ed. (London: Inter-Varsity, 1952), p. 182.
19. Duncan, pp. 138-41.

connotation is "hook."[20] Albright believed that was the real solution to the matter and identified it as a hook used in scaling ramparts.[21] The resultant translation, then, would be "whosoever getteth up by means of the hook and smiteth the Jebusites." The *New English Bible* follows Duncan and Albright by translating *tsinnor* as "grappling-iron."

Kathleen Kenyon, in her 1961-67 excavations at Jebusite Jerusalem, discovered that the city wall was not located as far up the slope of the hill as Duncan, Macalister, and others would have put it. Therefore, if Joab and his men had ascended the channel of the city water supply in their conquest of Jerusalem, they would have been able to enter the strategically important parts of town. And she concluded that David's men did indeed capture the city in this way when they made it the capital of Israel about 1000 B.C.[22]

Restoration of the Hebrew Commonwealth

In wrath God remembered mercy. Nestled in a context that announces captivity are Scripture passages promising protection and return to the land. Israel may have been unfaithful to her God, yet He, on His part, kept covenant with His chosen people and continued to shepherd the leaderless flock. Moreover, He was shaping the affairs of nations to prepare the way for their return to Palestine.

One of the greatest events that made possible the restoration was the death of Nebuchadnezzar. While his strong arm wielded the mace of power in Mesopotamia, there was little questioning of Babylon's authority. Upon his death, however, wholly inadequate rulers took his place, and the empire gradually grew weaker. Meanwhile a new empire was rising to the east—the Medo-Persian. Within that empire, Cyrus of Anshan rebelled against his Median overlords and at length overran all of Persia and Media, and the new Medo-Persian power took Babylon in 539 B.C. Now Cyrus was in a position to act as God's anointed (Isaiah 45:1) and perform the work of restoring the Jews.

It must not be supposed, however, that Cyrus was a pious worshiper of Yahweh simply because in Scripture he was called God's "anoint-

---

20. Ibid., p. 141.
21. William F. Albright, "The Old Testament and Archaeology," in *Old Testament Commentary*, ed. Herbert C. Alleman and Elmer E. Flack (Philadelphia: Muhlenberg, 1948), p. 149.
22. Kathleen Kenyon, *Royal Cities of the Old Testament* (New York: Shocken, 1971), pp. 24-27.

ed" and His "shepherd." The Lord often accomplishes His purposes through some very ungodly individuals. In this case, it should be noted that as soon as the Persian king entered Babylon, he built a shrine to the god Sin, and monuments that he erected during his lifetime attributed his long list of successes to Marduk.[23]

Nor was his kindliness toward the Jews an indication of his religious convictions, for at the outset of his reign he committed himself to a policy that called for returning captive gods to their temples and captive peoples to their homes. In his inscriptions he spoke of sending the gods of various peoples back to their shrines, and a line from the Cyrus Cylinder (discovered by H. Rassam in Babylon) states specifically, "I gathered together all their populations and restored (them to) their dwelling places."[24] This was a reversal of the Assyrian and Babylonian idea of deporting subjugated peoples from their homes and sending others to take the place of the captives. Cyrus was thus in a much better position to secure the good will, rather than the fear, of his subjects. No doubt the Persian king issued separate edicts to the various conquered nations, permitting them to return to their homes. Probably part of the Jewish decree is copied in Ezra 1:2-4, and additional specifications included in the document may be referred to in Ezra 3:2-7; 5:13-16; and 6:1-5.

As already mentioned, Cyrus was not particularly worshipful of Yahweh. Certain reasons, however, in addition to that of his general clemency, may have led him to make the declaration for the Jews to return to Palestine: (1) It may be that someone showed him the prophecy in Isaiah 44 and 45, as Josephus suggests.[25] (2) Palestine was a good buffer state between southwestern Asia and Egypt, and it would be advantageous to him to have an ally in this area. (3) It also relieved him of a dissatisfied element of his population, for since all Jews were invited to return to their homeland it would be evident to them that Cyrus desired to care for them and wanted to rebuild their inheritance. At any rate, the Jews did return, some 50,000 strong (Ezra 2), in 538-537 B.C. They carried with them vessels of the temple and many gifts from the Persians (Ezra 1:6-7). Although great vicissitudes still lay

23. A. T. Olmstead, *History of Palestine and Syria* (Grand Rapids: Baker, 1965), pp. 553-55.
24. Ibid., p. 555; Ira M. Price, Ovid R. Sellers, and E. Leslie Carlson, *The Monuments and the Old Testament* (Philadelphia: Judson, 1958), pp. 313-14.
25. Flavius Josephus *Antiquities of the Jews* 11:1, 1-2.

before them, the initial steps had been taken, and eventually the temple and walls were completed. To be sure, many Persian rulers were involved in the process, but Cyrus, God's anointed, made the original decree permitting the restoration, and his gifts gave impetus to the recovery. He accomplished all that the Scripture claimed for him.

8

Archaeology and Bible Kings

According to Robert Dick Wilson, the names of twenty-six foreign kings recorded in the Old Testament have been found on documents contemporary with the kings. In addition, the names of six kings of Israel and four of Judah have been located in Assyrian records.[1] When the results of New Testament study and further Old Testament investigation since the days of Wilson's publication (1926) are added to the thirty-six that he reports, the total number must approach fifty. It would seem apparent, then, that an entire volume or two could be profitably devoted to the study of archaeology and Bible kings; however, only five are chosen here in an effort to demonstrate by example the possibilities of a study of this field.

The Glories of Solomon's Reign

For almost three millennia Solomon has been renowned for his wisdom and splendor. To the Jews his name speaks of the zenith of their history; to the believer it is a name that at once spells achievement under the blessing of God and symbolizes practices to be avoided in one's personal life. To the destructive higher critic the scriptural account of his glory is to be taken with three grains of salt; to the Bible believer it is true.

1. Robert D. Wilson, *A Scientific Investigation of the Old Testament* (Chicago: Moody, 1959), pp. 72-73, 81.

Scripture points out that Solomon carried on extensive building projects: "And this is the reason of the levy which king Solomon raised; for to build the house of the LORD, and his own house, and Millo, and the wall of Jerusalem, and Hazor, and Megiddo, and Gezer" (1 Kings 9:15). His navy plied the seas: "And king Solomon made a navy of ships in Ezion-geber, which is beside Eloth, on the shore of the Red Sea, in the land of Edom" (1 Kings 9:26). His income ("Now the weight of gold that came to Solomon in one year was six hundred threescore and six talents of gold," 1 Kings 10:14) supported such programs as the establishment of strong defenses: "And Solomon gathered together chariots and horsemen; and he had a thousand and four hundred chariots, and twelve thousand horsemen, whom he bestowed in the cities for chariots, and with the king at Jerusalem" (1 Kings 10:26).

The extent of the kingdom. "Solomon reigned over all kingdoms from the river unto the land of the Philistines, and unto the border of Egypt; they brought presents and served Solomon all the days of his life"(1 Kings 4:21). The region delineated in this verse is roughly four hundred miles from north to south. Such a fact poses a problem, for the Syro-Palestine area had long resounded with the hoofbeats of horses and the tramping of soldiers of Egyptian, Mesopotamian, and other powers, as they sought to extend the borders of their empires.

Could Solomon in 950 B.C. have ruled such a large area? A study of archaeology and ancient history provides the answer. The Egyptian Empire was in a period of decline, which began about 1150 B.C. During succeeding centuries her previous glory faded, and most of the revivals of power in that nation were accomplished by foreign rulers. However, not even one of these did much for Egypt until the days of Shishak I (or Sheshonk I), approximately 945-924 B.C. In Assyria, after a drive for empire by Tiglath-pileser I (about 1100 B.C.), military strength declined and remained in a decadent condition until approximately 875 B.C. The Hittite Empire, which had controlled Asia Minor and north Syria, came to an end shortly after 1200 B.C. Soon thereafter Mycenean states of Greece lost their naval and commercial prominence in the eastern Mediterranean world and collapsed. Thus a rare opportunity for expansion was afforded the two great Hebrew monarchs, David and Solomon, and an answer is provided for those who have said it was impossible for Israel to expand in the Near East at that time because she was surrounded by great powers.

The Fortress Cities

The specific example of Megiddo. For the most part Solomon inherited the Hebrew Empire from his father, David, but it fell to Solomon's lot to fortify and improve the land that came under his suzerainty. Apparently he sought faithfully to discharge this responsibility, for 1 Kings 9:15 mentions that he fortified such sites as Jerusalem, Hazor, Gezer, and Megiddo.

Excavations at Megiddo (Tel el-Mutesellim) have been especially concerned with Solomon's activities there. Work at the site proved to be one of the greatest archaeological tasks ever undertaken. Although the German Oriental Society began preliminary investigations there (1903-1905), the most important excavation was carried on by the Oriental Institute of the University of Chicago according to a plan to devote twenty-five years to the complete excavation of the mound. Some idea of the magnitude of the endeavor is gained from the fact that the area of the summit of the tell amounted to about fifteen acres, with the slopes comprising thirty-five more; and the stratification extended to a depth of as much as seventy-two feet. The first fourteen years of the work occupied the seasons of 1925 to 1939; excavation was curtailed by World War II. Successive directors of the expedition were Clarence Fisher, P. L. O. Guy, and Gordon Loud.

The excavators identified Stratum IV as the Solomonic level at Megiddo. The top of the stratum consisted almost entirely of public buildings; but two stable compounds, holding about 450 horses, covered approximately a fifth of the area of the city. Evidence seemed to indicate that the domestic area lay outside the walls and that this was just the fortress.

But since the excavations of Yigael Yadin at Megiddo (1960, 1965-67), there has been a modification of the conclusions of the University of Chicago team.[2] The city wall, the massive city gate, and the palace in the southern part of the tell are still assigned to Solomon. The great water system (in the southwest corner of the mound), previously dated to the twelfth century, has been attributed to Solomon and his successors. And the stables have been assigned to Ahab.

The city wall, extending around the entire perimeter of the flat top of the mound, measured about 890 yards. Its thickness was some

2. Yigael Yadin, "New Light on Solomon's Megiddo," *Biblical Archaeologist*, 1960, pp. 62-68; see also Yadin, "Megiddo," *Encyclopedia of Archaeological Excavations in the Holy Land*, 3:853-56.

eleven feet in most places, but near the main gate it was slightly thicker; there is no evidence of its height. The corners of the wall were of drafted ashlar blocks, but the straight stretches consisted of roughly coursed rubble. Traces of an outer fortification wall around the foot of the mound were also found, dating back to this period.

Moving from a discussion of the walls of the city, one logically turns next to a consideration of the gate. This was built of three rows of hewn stone in the lower courses, the upper part being constructed of mud-brick—a characteristic of much of Solomonic fortification. The gate was double. If an enemy forced its way through the outer gate, it would find itself in a small paved enclosure and confronted by the masonry of the main gate into the city. Both outer and inner gates had guard rooms on either side.

The employment of "three rows of hewn stone" in the Megiddo gate throws interesting light on 1 Kings 7:12, where Solomon's house is described as having "three rows of hewed stones, and a row of cedar beams." Moreover, Guy, in speaking of Megiddo houses, noted that wherever a third layer of stones was preserved, the top of them was burned black; and in one case when a charred chunk of wood was analyzed by the Palestine Department of Agriculture it proved to be cedar. Guy felt that this demonstrated a north Syrian influence.[3] Phoenician architecture of Solomon's time used this style of construction, and it must be remembered that Solomon and Hiram of Tyre carried on extensive commercial relationships.

Located in the southern portion of the city was the palace. The dimensions of this edifice were twenty-five yards east and west and slightly less than that north and south. Along the northern half of the east face was a porch projecting about nine yards. A similar but smaller porch was located on the west side of the building. The depth of the foundation of the walls shows the structure to have been quite tall.

The water system at Megiddo is one of the most impressive in Palestine. The ancient engineers cut a diagonal shaft 81 feet down into the tell and from the bottom of this shaft a 224-foot tunnel through the rock to tap a spring outside the city. Then they covered the spring so attackers would not suspect its existence.

Other sites. In addition to the site of Tell el-Mutesellim, other excavations have added their testimony concerning the fortresses of

3. P. L. O. Guy, *New Light From Armageddon* (Chicago: U. of Chicago, 1931), pp. 34-35.

Solomon. Gezer and Hazor appear along with Megiddo in 1 Kings 9:15 as cities that Solomon fortified. Though much is left to be done at Gezer, a Solomonic gate complex virtually identical with that of Megiddo has been found there.[4]

John Garstang began excavation at Hazor in 1926, but Yigael Yadin launched more definitive campaigns there in 1955 through 1958 and 1968. Although the site consists of a large rectangular area and its adjacent tell, only the twenty-five-acre tell was occupied during the Solomonic period. Abandoned after the Hebrew conquest, Hazor was not reoccupied until Solomon's day. Then the Hebrew king built up only the western portion of the tell. The wall complex is fifteen feet thick and has a magnificent gateway within which were located some official structures.[5] Later Ahab greatly expanded Solomon's administrative post at Hazor and turned it into a fine fortified center replete with an impressive water system similar to that of Megiddo.

Additional comments on Solomon's military preparations could be made, but perhaps a general statement by Adams will suffice. "Of great interest was the system of fortresses: Hazor guarded the strategic point in northern Canaan; Megiddo stood across the open plain of Esdraelon; Beth-horon blocked the dangerous pass to Jerusalem by way of Aijalon; Baalath stood on the connecting highway from Jerusalem to the seaport of Joppa; Gezer protected the main road and entrance to the valley of Sorek; Tamar occupied a point on the southern borders to defend caravans from the ports of Ezion-geber and Elath. It is significant that in this system of defense no fortress was located east of Jerusalem, the Valley of Jordan being regarded as sufficient barrier."[6]

Solomon at Jerusalem

At Jerusalem Solomon received tremendous incomes. He took in 666 gold talents a year, in addition to taxes on commerce (1 Kings 10:14). To discover the comparative value of that amount, one would have to multiply the weight of the Israelite talent (about seventy-five pounds) by whatever gold is worth on the world market on a given day. His construction included the Temple and his palace, the former taking seven years to complete and the latter thirteen years. For this

---

4. Kathleen Kenyon, *Royal Cities of the Old Testament* (New York: Shocken, 1971), p. 69.
5. Ibid., pp. 57-58; Yigael Yadin, *Hazor* (London: Weidenfeld & Nicolson, 1975).
6. J. M. Adams, *Biblical Backgrounds*, rev. J. A. Callaway (Nashville: Broadman, 1965), p. 111.

work he used Phoenician workers. The Temple with its courts covered an area of thirty-five acres; and the palace consisted of a complex of closely connected buildings, including what may have been an armory, a throne room, a private residence for the king, and a separate house for the daughter of the Pharaoh of Egypt. In addition, he incorporated the Temple area into the city and extended the walls to include almost all the southwest hill. Walls have been found there that may have been the work of Solomon.[7]

The King's Seaport

From 1938 to 1940 Nelson Glueck excavated at Tell el-Kheleifeh near the modern Israeli port of Eilat on the Gulf of Aqaba and identified it as Solomon's seaport of Ezion-geber. The wall, two and one-half to three yards thick with a foundation course which extended about a yard below the soil, was built of sun-dried brick and was originally easily twenty-five feet high. Near the southwest corner of the town and facing the sea stood the triple gate. The first two gates opened into separate sets of guard rooms and the third into the main street of town. Only about an acre and a half lay within the walls.

Built on virgin soil, Ezion-geber was constructed at one time from a carefully worked out plan.[8] Hundreds of workmen would have been needed to build the site, and providing transportation and supplies for them was a feat in itself.

One of the most spectacular finds at Tell el-Kheleifeh was a forty-by-forty-foot structure that Glueck identified as "the finest and largest smelting and refining plant ever discovered in the ancient Near East."[9] This he related to a highly developed copper industry involving several mining sites and smelters extending from the Dead Sea to the Red Sea and dating to the days of Solomon.[10] The exciting story that Glueck pieced together on the basis of his explorations and excavations was presented in the scholarly literature on Palestine and became part of the proud reciting of heritage by the Israeli Ministry of Tourism.

But with the passage of time questions began to arise concerning this

---

7. Jack Finegan, *Light from the Ancient Past*, 2d ed. (Princeton: Princeton U., 1959), p. 179.
8. Nelson Glueck, "Ezion-Geber," *Bulletin of the American Schools of Oriental Research*, October 1939, p. 10.
9. Ibid.
10. Nelson Glueck, *The Other Side of Jordan* (New Haven, Conn.: Amer. School of Oriental Res., 1940), pp. 60-61.

whole reconstruction. In 1965 Professor Glueck himself recognized that the "blast furnace" at Tell el-Kheleifeh was something quite different—a citadel that was also used as a storehouse or granary.[11] Meanwhile Benno Rothenberg of Tel Aviv University, Glueck's assistant and chief photographer, had been working on the copper sites of the area between the Dead Sea and the Gulf of Aqaba, and he excavated in the region from 1964 to 1970. Probably his most significant single find came in 1969, when he was working at Timna, about twenty miles north of Eilat. There he uncovered a temple used by both the Egyptians and Midianites of the area and dating to about 1300 B.C., as proved by inscriptions from the reigns of the Egyptian rulers Seti I and Raamses II. The temple was dedicated to Hathor, the Egyptian goddess of mining. Rothenberg concluded that the copper industry of the region was a result of Egyptian-Midianite cooperation of the thirteenth century B.C. and was not Solomonic.[12] In fact, Rothenberg is convinced that this area was never mined for copper in Solomon's time.[13] Moreover, he believes that Tell el-Kheleifeh is not to be identified with Ezion-geber. The tell lies five hundred yards from the shoreline, which has not shifted since 1000 B.C. and apparently did not have port facilities.[14] Some scholars would put Ezion-geber on an island, Jezirat Far 'un, just south of Eliat along the Sinai coast.

The Royal Navy

"And king Solomon made a navy of ships in Ezion-geber, which is beside Eloth, on the shore of the Red Sea, in the land of Edom. And Hiram sent in the navy his servants, shipmen that had knowledge of the sea, with the servants of Solomon" (1 Kings 9:26-27). Since coastal lands between Carmel and Gaza did not offer a single harbor suitable for seagoing vessels in the days of the kings of Israel, Solomon felt compelled to establish a seaport at Ezion-geber, a site that had more possibilities from a natural standpoint. Nothing much is known about the navy Solomon built, but more than likely the ships were of

11. Nelson Glueck, "Transjordan," in *Archaeology and Old Testament Study*, ed. D. Winton Thomas (Oxford: Clarendon, 1967), pp. 438-39.
12. Lecture by Benno Rothenberg in Tel Aviv, June 21, 1972; and Jerry M. Landay, *Silent Cities, Sacred Stones* (New York: McCall, 1970), pp. 110-13. See also Rothenberg, *Were These King Solomon's Mines?* (New York: Stein & Day, 1972).
13. Landay, p. 164.
14. Ibid., p. 165.

Phoenician style. Ezion-geber became the marketplace for caravans moving from Arabia to Palestine. Caravans also carried important materials from Ezion-geber to Jerusalem, via Tamar in the wilderness.

It might be interesting to note in passing that the Phoenicians would have had no opposition to Solomon's construction of a merchant marine, because all of his trade was oriented toward the Red Sea and the East. As long as there was no Suez Canal, it would be impossible for Solomon to challenge Phoenician supremacy in the Mediterranean. Moreover, Tyre stood to gain by selling maritime knowledge to the Hebrew monarch and at the same time acquiring through him rare oriental products that could be used in her Mediterranean trade.

Glueck believes that Solomon's trade became so tremendous that it seriously affected the prosperity of the Queen of Sheba, so much so that she came to him to arrange trade agreements. "When one realizes what a terrifically hard journey it must have been for this fair ruler of a rich part of Southern Arabia, to come by camel a distance of some 1200 miles or more on her famous trip to Jerusalem to see Solomon, it is hard to believe that she undertook the long and arduous journey merely to bask in the brilliance of the king of Jerusalem."[15]

Shishak Invades Judah

Before Solomon died, a rift developed between him and Jeroboam, who had been an official in the department of public works; and the latter found it more convenient to leave the country, so he went to Egypt. Upon his return, disruption of the Hebrew kingdom occurred; and Jeroboam assumed headship of the northern tribes, while Rehoboam became king of Judah. Amid conflicts between Israel and Judah, Shishak I of Scripture (1 Kings 14:25; 2 Chronicles 12:2) or Sheshonk I of Egyptian records (founder of the twenty-second dynasty) took advantage of Hebrew weakness and invaded Judah in the fifth year of Rehoboam's reign. According to Thiele, this event probably took place in 925 B.C.[16]

The Bible narrative intimates a rather crushing defeat, for Shishak was able to carry off the treasures of the Temple and palace; but Egyptian records point to more far-reaching disaster. On a wall in the

15. Glueck, *The Other Side of Jordan*, p. 85.
16. E. R. Thiele, *The Mysterious Numbers of the Hebrew Kings*, new rev. ed. (Grand Rapids: Zondervan, 1982), p. 56.

Karnak temple, Shishak inscribed a relief depicting 156 captives taken in this campaign. They are led by cords clasped in the hand of the god Amun, and on the body of each captive appears a Palestinian place name; so we have there a listing of the towns the Egyptian king took during his Judean conquests. At present about one hundred twenty of the names are legible, but by no means can all of them be identified geographically. Some of the more important that can be recognized are Megiddo, Gibeon, Taanach, Beth-shean, and Ajalon.[17] Evidently Shishak sacked scores of towns in both the Northern and Southern kingdoms.

The King Who Took Samaria

Clouds of doom hovered over Israel almost from the inception of the divided monarchy. True, there were times of economic prosperity when Omri built Samaria and Ahab constructed his "ivory" palace and the kings enjoyed the income from the rich farming area of northern Palestine; but Jeroboam's idolatrous act of setting up the golden calves at Dan and Bethel and Ahab's introduction of Baal worship could only incur the eventual wrath of God. Moreover, it is said that all of the kings of Israel walked in the steps of Jeroboam, and certainly their subjects shared in their evil practices. Since Assyria was the most powerful northern neighbor of Israel, it was from that quarter that trouble could be expected.

Assyrian contact with Israel began in 853 B.C., when Shalmaneser III fought the Syro-Palestine confederacy allied against him at Qarqar. At that time ten thousand of Ahab's troops met defeat, as the Monolith Inscription of Shalmaneser indicates. Following him, Jehu paid tribute to Shalmaneser, a fact that is demonstrated by an inscription on the Black Obelisk of Shalmaneser. Between 782 and 745 B.C., Assyrian kings were mediocre, and their inactivity in the west gave courage to Judah and Israel and surrounding nations. Then Assyrian power was felt once more. In 738 B.C. Menahem was forced to pay tribute to Tiglath-pileser III (744-727 B.C.); and six years later, in response to the plea of Ahaz, the Judean, the Assyrian swooped down on the Northern Kingdom, taking Gilead, Galilee, and Naphtali, carrying their inhabitants to Assyria (2 Kings 15:29). This action is confirmed by Assyrian records.

17. Finegan, p. 113.

Shalmaneser V succeeded Tiglath-pileser in 727 B.C. Hoshea of Israel, along with other satellite nations, entertained ideas of revolt. Soon, however, the new king was on the job, and a three-year siege of Samaria began. At length the city was taken, but the Bible does not indicate the name of the instigator of the siege or the victor, or whether there was a change of rulers during it. While there is still some controversy over the matter, most biblical scholars conclude that Shalmaneser V began this siege and that he died in 722. At that time Sargon II (722-705 B.C.) took the throne, and the city fell during the first year of his reign. Very probably the truth of the matter is that the same army that invested the city also secured its surrender, neither the army nor the inhabitants of Samaria knowing much, if anything, about the change of rulers. Some argue rather forcefully that Samaria actually fell during the last days of Shalmaneser's reign.

Sargon has left us his own description of the victory, which reads as follows: "I besieged and captured Samaria, carrying off 27,290 of the people who dwelt therein. 50 chariots I gathered from among them, I caused others to take their (the deported inhabitants') portion, I set my officers over them and imposed upon them the tribute of the former king."[18] Revealed here is the Assyrian's apparent unconcern for the importance of this event. Comments Caiger: "Thus briefly and unimaginatively the Assyrian records his subjugation of one of the most notable cities in history. To him the kingdom of Israel was but one of a hundred petty outlying states, and its royal capital but one of a thousand unimportant towns to be squeezed of all possible spoil and then crushed under foot. . . . But to the Jews themselves, the fall of Samaria was the work not of Sargon, whose name they disdained even to record, but of the Providence of Jehovah, a dreadful warning of the inevitable effect of apostasy and evil deeds."[19]

Assyrian Attack Repulsed

When the Assyrians completed their conquest of the northern tribes, they continued their march south into Judah. Scripture states that in the fourteenth year of Hezekiah, king of Judah (701 B.C.),

18. Daniel D. Luckenbill, *Ancient Records of Assyria and Babylon*, 2 vols. (Westport, Conn.: Greenwood, 1968), 2:26.
19. S. L. Caiger, *Bible and Spade* (New York: Oxford U., 1951), pp. 148-49.

Sennacherib "came up against all the defensed cities of Judah, and took them" (Isaiah 36:1). Extended accounts in Kings and Chronicles detail events of the campaign: the general success of Sennacherib, the threats of the Assyrian hosts, the illness of Hezekiah, Hezekiah's initial fear but ultimate trust in God, and Sennacherib's defeat by means of a divinely sent plague of some sort.

Interesting confirmation of Sennacherib's part in this venture appears in two virtually identical inscriptions on clay cylinders found in his palace at Nineveh. One of these is in the British Museum in London and the other in the Oriental Institute Museum of the University of Chicago. Luckenbill translates:

> As for Hezekiah, the Jew, who did not submit to my yoke, 46 of his strong, walled cities, as well as the small cities in their neighborhood, which were without number—by escalade and by bringing up siege engines (?), by attacking and storming on foot, by mines, tunnels, and breaches (?), I besieged and took (those cities). 200,150 people, great and small, male and female, horses, mules, asses, camels, cattle and sheep, without number, I brought away from them and counted as spoil. Himself, like a caged bird, I shut up in Jerusalem, his royal city. Earthworks I threw up against him,—the one coming out of his city gate I turned back to his misery. The cities of his, which I had despoiled, I cut off from his land. . . . As for Hezekiah, the terrifying splendor of my majesty overcame him, and the Urbi (Arabs) and his mercenary (?) troops which he had brought in to strengthen Jerusalem, his royal city, deserted him (*lit.*, took leave)."[20]

It is very revealing to see the attitude of Sennacherib here. Obviously, something happened at Jerusalem to keep him from capturing the city; his statement proves he did not take it. In an effort to cover up his defeat, he made the best of a bad situation and played up the successes he did have. Nowhere did he claim conquest of Jerusalem. On this same invasion of Judah, Sennacherib was successful in conquering Lachish and memorialized the fact by devoting a couple of walls of his palace in Nineveh to a pictorial representation of the siege and capture of the city (now on display in the British Museum). Conquest of Jerusalem and destruction of the Judean kingdom would have prompted a much more grandiose artistic celebration.

---

20. Luckenbill, 2:120-21.

Josiah's Defeat and Death

Shortly before the fall of the kingdom of Judah, an event took place that raises several questions in the mind of the casual reader; but viewed against a backdrop of history now available as a result of Near Eastern studies, it makes a good deal of sense. The event was the attack by Josiah of Judah on Pharaoh Necho of Egypt.

The record in 2 Kings 23:29 relates, "In his days Pharaoh-nechoh king of Egypt went up against the king of Assyria to the river Euphrates: and king Josiah went against him; and he slew him at Megiddo, when he had seen him." Immediately the question arises, Why should Josiah go to war with someone who was on his way to attack a traditional enemy of Judah? For the answer, we must look at the international situation.

To begin with, it is necessary to place this event chronologically. Generally accepted chronology pegs the death of Josiah in 609 B.C. A reconstruction based on archaeological discoveries demonstrates that by that time Assyrian power was decadent. Egypt had shaken herself loose from Assyrian suzerainty and entertained grandiose ideas of taking control in Palestine; Nabopolassar had set up an independent state at Babylon (625 B.C.); and a coalition of Medes, Babylonians, and Scythians had toppled Nineveh, capital of the empire (612 B.C.). Meanwhile, Josiah was engaged in religious reforms (2 Kings 22-23) and had even succeeded in making his power felt throughout the three Assyrian provinces on the north, which once constituted the kingdom of Israel. It is not unthinkable that Josiah had made some sort of league with the Babylonians, as did Hezekiah before him.

Though Nineveh was lost, the Assyrian Empire was still a going concern. Troops held out at Carchemish in the west. Now Pharaoh Necho was going north, apparently with the intention of helping the Assyrians against their foes. Josiah felt impelled to act, possibly for three reasons: (1) Jewish territory was being violated, (2) his alliance with Babylon obligated him to do so, and (3) Assyria, his great enemy, would no doubt be destroyed if deprived of the aid of Egypt.

It should be noted that the Hebrew word for *against* in 2 Kings 23:29 can be interpreted to mean either "to oppose" or "to aid." The latter is correct in connection with Necho's action and the former with Josiah's. In other words, Necho sought to aid Assyria, while Josiah tried to prevent the aid from arriving. The *New International Version* properly translates, "Pharaoh Neco king of Egypt went up to help the king of Assyria." For his trouble Josiah met death at the hands of the Egyptians, who then marched north and joined an Assyrian force in attacking Babylonians stationed at Haran in northern Mesopotamia. But the Babylonians were destined to crush all pockets of Assyrian resistance, as well as Necho's army, within a couple of years after the death of the Hebrew king.[21]

From Assyria, Egypt, Palestine, Persia, Rome, and many areas of lesser importance comes information dealing with kings mentioned in the Bible. New light concerning these men has proved to be supplementary to the Scripture rather than contradictory to it, and the continuing discoveries are very beneficial in reconstructing a more well-rounded view of cultural and historical developments in Bible times.

---

21. Frank Cross and David Freedman, "Josiah's Revolt Against Assyria," *Journal of Near Eastern Studies,* January 1953, pp. 56-58.

9

Archaeology and Bible Cities

Abraham's Hometown

For millennia the name *Abraham* has stirred the religious sensitivities of Jew, Christian, and Muslim alike; for all three great monotheistic religions claim a relationship to him. Therefore, no study of archaeology, however brief, would seem complete without some reference to the "father of the faithful."

According to Genesis 11, Abraham was born in Ur of the Chaldees and spent his early life there, until after his marriage. Though once an important city, Ur gradually disappeared from history sometime after the days of Cyrus the Great (sixth century B.C.), as a result of a change in the course of the Euphrates River, which left the area without adequate water for irrigation. Even the site of the famous metropolis was unknown until 1854, when J. E. Taylor excavated briefly at Tell Mukayyar, 150 miles northwest of the Persian Gulf, and identified it as Ur. In 1918, R. Campbell Thompson conducted further work there under the auspices of the British Museum, to be followed later in the same year by an expedition led by H. R. Hall, representing the same institution. The main work at the site, however, was done by a joint expedition of the University Museum of Philadelphia and the British Museum in a protracted excavation headed by Sir Leonard Woolley (1922-34).

Since discoveries at Ur[1] revealed more than one period of occupation, it becomes necessary to determine the one with which Abraham should be associated. The Hebrew text points to the fact that the patriarchs sojourned in Canaan for 215 years (Genesis 21:5; 25:26; 47:9),[2] and their descendants were in Egypt 430 years more (Exodus 12:40-41). If those two figures are added to an approximate 1440 B.C. date for the Exodus, Abraham would have entered Canaan about 2085 B.C. Since he was seventy-five when he left Haran for Canaan (Genesis 12:4), he would have been born about 2160 B.C. A glance at Mesopotamian developments of that period reveal that the hated Guti were in the land. That little-known Caucasian people from the mountains east of Mesopotamia controlled the Tigris-Euphrates Valley from 2180 to 2070 B.C., according to the minimal chronology that was proposed by Albright, Finegan, and others and is now becoming quite widely accepted.[3] Acceptance of one of the slightly different chronologies for the Guti period would still find them in control at the time of Abraham's birth.

How soon after his birth Abraham left Ur is not known; but if one follows Finegan's chronology for Ur's golden age (2070-1960 B.C.), the departure occurred before Ur entered that age. Woolley then would have been in error in popularizing the view that Abraham's days in Ur coincided with the city's greatest days.[4] It should be noted, however, that other chronologies give variant dates for Ur's ascendancy, and a choice of an earlier set of dates makes possible Abraham's residence in the metropolis then. For example, Roebuck dates the period 2135-2027 B.C.[5] Whenever it happened, Terah's resettlement with his son at Haran

---

1. Although Cyrus Gordon has argued for the location of the Ur which was Abraham's birthplace in northern Mesopotamia ("Abraham and the Merchants of Ura," *Journal of Near Eastern Studies*, January 1958, p. 30), his view has not met with wide acceptance. H. F. W. Saggs answered Gordon in "Ur of the Chaldees, a Problem of Identification," *Iraq*, 1960, 22: 200-209.
2. These references show that Abraham was 75 when he moved into Canaan and 100 when Isaac was born; Isaac was 60 when Jacob was born; and Jacob was 130 when he and his family moved to Egypt. Thus a total of 215 years elapsed while the patriarchs were in Canaan.
3. William F. Albright, "A Third Revision of the Early Chronology of Western Asia," *Bulletin of the American Schools of Oriental Research*, December 1942, p. 32; Jack Finegan, *Light from the Ancient Past*, 2d ed. (Princeton: Princeton U., 1959), p. 48.
4. See Charles Leonard Woolley, *Ur of the Chaldees* (Harmondsworth, Middlesex: Penguin, 1950), revised by P. R. S. Moorey (London: Herbert, 1982); and *Abraham: Recent Discoveries and Hebrew Origins* (New York: Scribner's, 1936).
5. Carl Roebuck, *The World of Ancient Times* (New York: Scribner's, 1966), p. 33.

is not surprising because it, like Ur, was a great center for the worship of the moon god Nanna.

If one follows the rendering of the Septuagint (Greek version of the Old Testament), however, he arrives at a far different conclusion for the date of Abraham. In the Septuagint rendering of Exodus 12:40 the 430 years are made to include the 215 years of patriarchal sojourn in Canaan, as well as the bondage in Egypt. Therefore the date of Abraham's birth must be pulled down 215 years, to 1945 B.C.—at the end of Ur's golden age.

To complicate matters even further, if one follows the Septuagint rendering of Exodus 12:40 and accepts a late date for the Exodus, about 1275 B.C., he would pull the birth of Abraham down another 165 years, to 1780 B.C. That would put Abraham's entrance into Canaan during the great days of Hammurabi. This writer feels that such a late date is unwarranted both because the early date of the Exodus is to be preferred and because historical conditions of the Palestine-Syrian area during the twentieth century B.C. more nearly fit the Abrahamic narrative as presented in Genesis.

It seems impossible at present to assign an exact date to Abraham's days at Ur. But taking everything into consideration, perhaps we are not far off in concluding with many Bible students of our day that he may have known the city during her days of greatest glory.

Long before the days of Abraham, Ur boasted a high development of civilization. Among the most remarkable discoveries made there by Woolley were the royal tombs, now dated by many scholars at about 2500 B.C. Since those ancient people had a strong belief in the afterlife, royalty was provided with all that might make such existence more pleasant. Musical instruments, jewelry, clothing, utensils of various kinds, wagons and beasts of burden, weapons, and even servants were placed in the tombs. King A-bar-gi's grave included sixty-five people besides himself; Queen Puabi's (formerly rendered Shubad) contained twenty-five.[6] Evidence of violent death being absent, it is supposed that those servants were either poisoned or drugged and buried alive.

It is impossible to describe here all the tombs excavated or the richness of the contents. The gold vases of Queen Puabi, the gold helmet of Meskalamdug, the elaborate headdresses of valuable metals and precious stones, the copper weapons and utensils all bespeak a high

6. Finegan, p. 41.

point of development in the civilization of Ur long before the days of Abraham. Woolley comments,

> The contents of the tombs illustrate a very highly developed state of society of an urban type, a society in which the architect was familiar with all the basic principles of construction known to us today. The artist, capable at times of a most vivid realism, followed for the most part standards and conventions whose excellence had been approved by many generations working before him; the craftsman in metal possessed a knowledge of metallurgy and a technical skill which few peoples ever rivaled; the merchant carried on a far-flung trade and recorded his transactions in writing; the army was well organized and victorious, agriculture prospered, and great wealth gave scope to luxury . . . and as has been demonstrated . . . this civilisation was already many centuries old.[7]

Suppose Abraham did know Ur during her golden age. Then Ur-Nammu was the guiding light to prosperity. Under him the city with its far-flung suburbs grew to be a flourishing metropolis, with the population of the built-up area in and around the city numbering in excess of 360,000 according to Woolley.[8] Her commercial influence was felt as far north as the Anatolian mountains, whence copper was secured, and for a great distance south along the Persian Gulf, where merchants obtained copper, gold, ivory, hard woods, and various types of stone. Within the city, factories produced textile and metal goods for export and home consumption. Fortunately for us, citizens of Ur made elaborate records of all their transactions. Bills of lading, invoices, letters of credit, court cases, tax records, and practice tablets of the schoolboy all came to light when the fingers of the excavator raised the curtain of time from the mound of Mukayyar.[9]

Building operations were tremendous during that period, too. Ur-Nammu constructed around the city proper a wall some two and one-half miles in circumference and seventy-seven feet thick. Within it, in the northwestern part, was the sacred, or Temenos, enclosure of the moon-god, Nanna, which measured about four hundred yards long and two hundred yards wide. Inside that enclosure stood the great brick ziggurat or stage-tower of Nanna, measuring about two hundred

---

7. Woolley, pp. 67-68.
8. Charles Leonard Woolley, *History of Mankind*, vol. 1, part 2 (New York: New American Library, 1965), 2:123-25.
9. Woolley, *Abraham*, pp. 118-33.

feet in length, one hundred fifty feet in width, and seventy feet in height. Each stage of the tower was smaller than the one below, and on the topmost level stood the temple of the god. Gardens were planted on the terraces. As was true of the Parthenon of Athens many centuries later, the ziggurat at Ur was without straight lines. By using ingeniously curved surfaces, the architects were able to create an appearance of elegance and grace not obtainable with straight lines.[10]

Education was also at a high stage of development in the twentieth century B.C. The "three R's" were basic, but one is particularly surprised by the great advancement in mathematics. Besides knowing the multiplication and division tables, the student was able to extract square and cube roots and do exercises in practical geometry.[11]

Turning briefly to a consideration of the dwellings of the period, Woolley remarks that they might measure about forty feet in width and fifty in depth and consist of two stories, the first for household tasks, storage, servant quarters, and the second for the family. They ranged in size from ten to twenty rooms, which were arranged around a central court open to the sky. With surprising modernity, the guest room was even adjoined by a lavatory.[12]

In spite of the fact that he might have had a share in all of this prosperity simply by returning to the home of the moon god, Abraham chose rather to walk with God in the poorer land of Canaan. But the Lord has His rewards for faithfulness; and there is evidence that the patriarch gained a good deal of wealth and prestige there, judging by the account of Genesis 14—to say nothing of the blessings promised through the Abrahamic covenant.

A Stronghold That Joshua Conquered

While Jericho may well be Palestine's oldest city, as is now commonly believed, the average Christian has no great interest in the early stages of the city's history. He almost always asks, "What about the days of Joshua?"

Excavations at Jericho (modern Telles-Sultan) were first carried on 1907 to 1909 by the German Oriental Society under the direction of

---

10. Woolley, *Ur of the Chaldees*, pp. 92-96.
11. Woolley, *Abraham*, p. 103.
12. Ibid., pp. 111-15.

Ernst Sellin and Carl Watzinger. They partially traced the history of the mound and outlined the city of Joshua's day, which proved to be only about eight acres in size—a solution to the query of the person who wonders how it would have been possible for the Israelites to get around the city seven times in one day, or even once a day.

John Garstang, supported financially by Sir Charles Marston, led the second expedition at Jericho in the years 1930-36. Garstang was able to complete the outline of the history of the mound that the Germans had begun, and he gave a good deal of attention to City D— the one destroyed by Joshua. He reported that the city had been surrounded by a double wall—the outer one six feet thick and the inner twelve feet thick—separated by a fifteen-foot space. Moreover, due to the crowded condition within the walls, houses were built upon them.

Garstang stated further that when the city fell to the Hebrews, the walls collapsed outward and slid down the slope on which the town was built. So completely were they destroyed that it would have been possible for attackers to climb over the rubble and into the city. In further confirmation of Scripture, the site was burned at the time of conquest. Moreover, as a result of Israelite obedience to God's prohibition against plundering the city, foodstuffs were found in abundance in the remains—a remarkable discovery when we consider that the Israelites had not yet had opportunity to raise crops since coming in from the desert. Furthermore, part of the wall next to the citadel still stood at a height of eighteen feet, a likely location for the house of Rahab. The walls originally may have been as high as thirty feet, and Garstang concluded that they fell about 1400 B.C.[13]

Several writers have suggested that an earthquake was responsible for the fall of the walls of Jericho. That is not beyond the realm of possibility, for there have been a number of destructive quakes in this general part of Palestine. The miracle, then, would not have been so much in the method of destruction as the timing—precisely the moment when the children of Israel finished the seventh trip around the city and gave their united shout.

The third Jericho expedition, a joint enterprise of the British School of Archaeology in Jerusalem and the American Schools of Oriental Research, was conducted 1952-58 under the leadership of Miss Kath-

13. John Garstang, *Joshua and Judges* (New York: Harper, 1931), pp. 145-47.

leen Kenyon, then director of the British School. Probably the most significant finds of the first three seasons of work come from the lowest, or prepottery, levels of Jericho and are therefore not of great concern to the Bible student. Since one of the main reasons for reopening the work at Jericho was to solve some of the problems of the Late Bronze Age level (time of Joshua), considerable attention was given to that stratum. Miss Kenyon concluded that Garstang erroneously had dated Early Bronze Age (3000-2000 B.C.) walls to the time of Joshua and that nothing remained of the walls of Joshua's day. She did, however, find some artifacts that she assigned to the city destroyed by Joshua and decided that the victorious attack of the Israelites occurred 1350-1325 B.C. The site gave no evidence of subsequent occupation until the days of Hiel the Bethelite, shortly after 900 B.C. (see 1 Kings 16:34).[14]

Apparently Garstang was wrong in identifying the walls he discovered as coming from the time of Joshua, so what he found should not be connected with either Joshua's conquest or the location of Rahab's house. That does not mean, however, that his conclusion about the 1400 B.C. date of the fall of the city has been entirely invalidated. In any case, only about fifty years separate Garstang's and Kenyon's positions as to when the city fell. In this connection, it is well to remember that pottery chronology does not permit exact dating. As far as the walls of Jericho in Joshua's day are concerned, we might postulate that they were made of mudbrick and that they eroded away during the four hundred to five hundred years the site was unoccupied. At least, neither Garstang nor Kenyon found them.

Capital on the Tigris

It was a dark day for Assyria when in August of 612 B.C. the capital of Nineveh fell to the combined forces of Medes, Babylonians, and Scythians. Another enemy of Israel met its doom under the judgment of God.[15] Soon thereafter the city disappeared from history, and its location was not even positively identified until 1847, during the excavations of A. H. Layard.[16] Subsequent and very fruitful work was carried on there in the last century by Layard, Hormuzd Rassam, and

14. Kathleen Kenyon, *Digging Up Jericho* (New York: Praeger, 1957), pp. 261-63.
15. See Nahum 3:1-3; Zephaniah 2:13-15.
16. Seton Lloyd, *Foundations in the Dust* (New York: Oxford U., 1949), p. 135.

George Smith for the British Museum, and Victor Place for the French. Further expeditions were sent to Nineveh by the British Museum in 1903 to 1905, led by L. W. King and R. C. Thompson, and in 1927-32, under the direction of R. Campbell Thompson and M. E. L. Mallowan. While the attention of the earlier excavators concentrated on the Great Assyrian period, Mallowan conducted a prehistoric sounding in the lower levels of the site. In 1954 the Department of Antiquities of Iraq excavated briefly at Nineveh.

Nineveh lay on the east bank of the Tigris and on the northwest corner of a plain about twenty-five by fifteen miles in extent, which was formed by the Tigris and its tributaries. Though the founding of the city took place before the days of Abraham, it did not become the capital of the Assyrian Empire until the days of Sennacherib (705-681 B.C.). To him goes the credit for the great city wall (measuring some eight miles in length and still standing to a height of twenty feet), and the Jerwan aqueduct, which brought water a distance of about thirty miles.

The fact that the walls were only eight miles in circumference has led Pfeiffer and others to argue against the accuracy of Jonah 3:3, where Nineveh is described as "an exceeding great city of three days' journey."[17] One way of dealing with the problem is to view the reference as including greater Nineveh, which with its suburbs may have stretched several miles to the north and more than twenty miles to the southeast, to Calah (Nimrud). Measured from end to end, that whole urban area would have extended over thirty miles. To go around it would have been a journey of more than sixty miles, or a three-day journey, at the rate of twenty miles a day. If the reference to 120,000 who did not know their right hand from their left (Jonah 4:11) had in view young children, then a total population of the built-up area may have been as much as 600,000 as is often asserted.

An alternate view is that Nineveh proper was such a large city that it would have taken three days to stop at its major centers to proclaim the judgment of God. On this supposition, the 120,000 might include the entire population, whose not knowing their right hand from their left is taken to indicate spiritual ignorance.

At present, Nineveh is represented by two great mounds—

17. Robert H. Pfeiffer, *Introduction to the Old Testament*, rev. ed. (New York: Harper & Row, 1948), p. 588.

Kouyunjik and Nebi Yunus (the prophet Jonah), and the site is so large that it may never be completely excavated. Most of the archaeological work in the past has been conducted at Kouyunjik, where Layard uncovered the palace of Sennacherib. This edifice contained seventy-one halls, chambers, and passages, almost all of which were covered with reliefs and inscriptions. By rough calculation, the reliefs totaled almost two miles in length.[18] Sennacherib, it will be remembered, invaded Judah in the days of Hezekiah, capturing dozens of towns and causing untold distress in the land, until the angel of death smote his forces while he attempted to take Jerusalem (2 Kings 18:17—19:37; Isaiah 36:37). Descriptions of events of this campaign have been found both in reliefs and inscriptions at his palace. Also of importance is substantial number of clay tablets found there.

Another extraordinary discovery made at Kouyunjik was the palace of Ashurbanipal (668-626 B.C.) and the royal library (see chapter 10). Although that Assyrian king does not figure prominently in the biblical narrative (except in Ezra 4:10, where he is called "Asnapper"), he does figure indirectly because of his passion for collecting copies of all extant literature. His copies of Flood epics and creation accounts are avidly studied by Bible scholars. Remains of a palace of Ashurnasirpal and construction by several other kings also have come to light on Kouyunjik.

Under surface of the mound of Nebi Yunus (so named because there is a tradition that Jonah's grave is there) lies the palace of Esarhaddon (681-668 B.C.); but since a modern town stands atop the tell, excavations have been very incomplete. The remaining acres of Nineveh's ruins await the further action of the archaeologist's pick before they relate to us the rest of the drama once enacted on that stage.

The Proud Crown of Ephraim

"Woe to the proud crown of the drunkards of Ephraim,"[19] cried the prophet Isaiah (Isaiah 28:1). Because Ephraim gradually assumed leadership over all the ten tribes, the prophets often addressed the Northern Kingdom as "Ephraim;" her "proud crown," then, was Samaria.

---

18. Lloyd, p. 139.
19. Franz Delitzsch, *Biblical Commentary on the Prophecies of Isaiah*, trans. Karl Friedrich Kiel (Grand Rapids: Eerdmans, 1949) 1:435.

Surely that city was the crown of Israel. Situated on an easily defensible hill three to four hundred feet above the fruitful plain and surrounded by a rich hinterland, Samaria was adorned by all the wealth and splendor her Hebrew royalty could shower upon her. Predictions of divine judgement against Samaria were fulfilled, however (as pointed out in the last chapter, where the conquests of Sargon of Assyria were described). Although subsequent rulers restored the site, the hill of Samaria today is uninhabited.

The first period of excavations of the northern capital was carried on from 1908 to 1910 under the direction of G. A. Reisner, C. S Fisher, and D. G. Lyon, sponsored by Harvard University. J. W. Crowfoot led a second expedition, 1931-33, in which Harvard, the Hebrew University in Jerusalem, the Palestine Exploration Fund, the British Academy, and the British School of Archaeology in Jerusalem cooperated. The last three organizations excavated at the site again in 1935.

Work at Samaria proved to be particularly fruitful in illuminating and confirming the biblical record. Omri and Ahab apparently leveled the top of the hill, which was previously uninhabited, as Scripture attests (1 Kings 16:24), surrounded the summit with a wall thirty-three feet thick in places, and began the palace compound. Originally the palace measured 160 feet square and was composed of a number of rooms arranged around open courts. Later kings enlarged the palace area greatly and built a second wall on the slope of the hill and a third at the base of it. In the palace grounds Reisner found a pool that may have been the pool of Samaria, where the bloodstained chariot of Ahab was washed (1 Kings 22:38). Numerous large cisterns turned up in the course of the excavations, revealing the source of water for the long sieges the city occasionally experienced.

The abundance of ivory, too, was an interesting discovery of the excavators. McCown notes that the 1935 expedition to Samaria found fragments of ivory spread over the entire city, and they were particularly thick near the center of the north city wall, where the "ivory house" may have been located.[20] Probably the "ivory house" was so called because the walls were thickly inlaid with carved ivory. Such a structure certainly would qualify for the biblical writer's description. Moreover, the excavators found many pieces of ivory inlay that once had been part of furniture; by these we are reminded of Amos's denunciation of the beds of ivory (Amos 6:4).

20. C. C. McCown, *The Ladder of Progress in Palestine* (New York: Harper, 1943), p. 197.

Light is shed on the economic and religious situation in the Northern Kingdom by the Samaria *ostraca*, about seventy in number. These are inscribed pieces of pottery dated by many to the reign of Jeroboam II in the early eighth century B.C. Since they were primarily tax and revenue receipts, they tell something of the economic situation of their time; their inscriptions provide information as to the science of Hebrew paleography of the eighth century B.C.; and the fact that many of the names found on them are compounds of *Baal* reveals the influence of Phoenician religion in Israel as a result of Jezebel's idolatrous efforts.

While the excavations show that a high point in the development of Old Testament Samaria was reached in the days of Jeroboam II, they point to another great period of glory during the reign of Herod the Great. Herod renamed the city "Sebaste," the Greek form of *Augustus*, in honor of the emperor, and beautified it greatly. He built a temple to Augustus on top of the ruins of the ancient Israelite palaces, a forum flanked by a basilica, a theater, an aqueduct, and a 900-yard long colonnaded street with adjacent shops.

Discoveries at Samaria reveal that the Northern Kingdom far exceeded the cultural developments of contemporary Judah; but she also outdistanced her southern neighbor in apostasy, and for this she first went into captivity.

The City Nebuchadnezzar Built

"Is not this the great Babylon I have built as the royal residence, by my mighty power and for the glory of my majesty?" asked Nebuchadnezzar as he walked in his garden one day (Daniel 4:30, NIV*). To a large degree his boast was true. Although Hammurabi (about 1700 B.C.) had raised the status of Babylon from that of an insignificant village to the position of foremost city of Babylonia and had engaged in building activities proportionate to her prestige, the city fell on evil days before the time of Nebuchadnezzar. In an effort to stop the constant rebellions of the Babylonians, Sennacherib of Assyria sacked the city in 690 B.C. and destroyed a large part of it. Esarhaddon (680-669 B.C.), son of Sennacherib, found that he could best placate his southern province by rebuilding Babylon. But it was Nebuchadnezzar II (605-562 B.C.) and his father, Nabopolassar (625-605 B.C.), who reconstructed the entire city along grander lines.

*New International Version.

Of the greatness that the city attained or the architectural monuments erected by Nebuchadnezzar, practically nothing was known, however, until the researches of Robert Koldewey, who excavated there for the German Oriental Society, 1899-1914. Since the earliest strata of occupation at Babylon now lie under water,[21] nearly everything found dated to the time of Nebuchadnezzar, except for one spot where a few houses of the Hammurabi period were reached.

Though the whole site had been plundered for brick and generally wrecked, it was possible for the expedition to recapture an accurate picture of the layout of the city, to outline its major buildings, procession street, and the famous Ishtar Gate. The double Ishtar Gate, with its flanking towers, was covered with shining blue glaze and ornamented with 575 yellow and white bulls and dragons executed in enameled brick. Through the gate passed the 75-foot wide Procession Street, which was paved with slabs of limestone and lined with sidewalks of red breccia. Surely this street was the scene of many great spectacles. Here trooped the captives, including Hebrews, whom Nebuchadnezzar took in war. Along the street, too, at the annual New Year festival, the image of Marduk was carried, and ritual acts were performed at each of the sacred buildings met en route. Surrounding the roughly rectangular city stood a wall that was eleven miles long and eighty-five feet thick and protected by a moat filled with water from the Euphrates. Actually the wall was double; the outer wall was twenty-five feet thick and the inner one twenty-three feet thick, with an intervening space filled with rubble.

One of the major structures of Babylon was the great ziggurat, or staged tower, some 295 feet high and composed of seven successively smaller stages, or stories.[22] On the topmost level stood a temple. In the eyes of many, the ziggurat at Babylon vies with that of nearby Birs Nimrud for the honor of possibly having been the biblical tower of Babel. A look at the facts, however, would not seem to allow the acceptance of such a theory. In the first place, the ziggurat at Babylon was enlarged by Nebuchadnezzar around 600 B.C. Granting that the structure he enhanced was erected by Hammurabi, the date of the ziggurat may be carried back to about 1700 B.C. If we allow further that Hammurabi may have known a small stage tower here before his day,

---

21. Sir Frederic Kenyon, *The Bible and Archaeology* (New York: Harper, 1940), p. 127.
22. André Parrot, *The Tower of Babel* (New York: Philosophical Library, 1955), p. 22.

we might possibly arrive at a date something like 2000 B.C. Earlier in this chapter reference was made to the ziggurat at Ur, constructed about 2000 B.C. by Ur-Nammu, possibly on top of a smaller tower dating three or four hundred years earlier. According to Parrot, more than thirty other Mesopotamian ziggurats are known to exist, the earliest true ziggurats dating to the third millennium B.C.[23] Now it must be admitted from archaeological evidence that there was a general diffusion of language in the Near East long before 3000 B.C.; therefore the tower of Babel described in Genesis 11 must have been constructed at a very early time—much earlier than any of the existing ziggurats. We might conjecture with Free[24] that these ziggurats known in later millennia of Mesopotamian history are descendants of the real tower of Babel, but certainly they are no more than that.

An evangelical who considers the suggestion that the ziggurat at Babylon is the tower of Babel must remember that such speculation has been launched by biblical scholars who believe that the Bible is a product of religious evolution and that some writer at a late date saw one of those towers in Babylonia and inserted the story in Genesis merely to explain the origin of the variety of languages in the world. To them, therefore, Genesis 11 is an etiological story (one invented to explain an origin) rather than real history. With such theorizing the conservative can have no sympathy. Moreover, one should take into account that the inhabitants of Mesopotamia came from the mountains to the east, and the ziggurats may have been an effort on their part to construct a man-made mountain in the plains so they might be nearer to their gods. In their original homes they had built high places in the mountains, which now had to be fashioned artificially.

The excavators explored five temples at Babylon, each surrounded by walled precincts. In every case temple gates opened on inner courts flanked by buildings. The shrine room with a raised dais for a cult statue was approached through an antechamber.

Nebuchadnezzar's palace was a huge complex of buildings protected by a double wall. Rooms of the palace surrounded five courtyards. The white-plastered throne room (55 by 170 feet) had a great central entrance flanked by smaller side doors.

Yet one more Babylonian structure deserves comment—the hanging

---

23. Ibid., pp. 26-43.
24. Joseph P. Free, *Archaeology and Bible History* (Wheaton, Ill.: Scripture Press, 1964), p. 46.

gardens, viewed by the Greeks as one of the seven wonders of the world. There is at present no absolute certainty as to their location. Some have felt that they may have been arranged on the stages of the ziggurat, as at Ur. Since Koldewey's location of the hanging gardens at the northeast corner of Nebuchadnezzar's palace has not been generally accepted, we still look for the site of that ancient wonder.

Such was Nebuchadnezzar's Babylon. It fell to the Medo-Persian combine in 539 B.C. and passed out of existence with the Tartar invasion of the area in the early thirteenth century of the Christian era. In fulfillment of prophecy it has become as Sodom (Isaiah 13:17-22).

Paul's Headquarters

Although most of the literature on Bible archaeology has dealt with the Old Testament, by virtue of the fact that thousands of years of history are covered by the Old Testament as opposed to fewer than a hundred years by the New, there should be a representation of New Testament archaeology in any introduction on the subject. Chapter 6 discussed the text of the New Testament. Now we take a glance at three important New Testament cities. And what better choices could we make than Antioch of Syria, Paul's headquarters; Ephesus, the scene of Paul's most extended evangelistic efforts; and Corinth, the site of his greatest European labors.

From Antioch, Paul launched all three of his missionary tours, and there he returned at the end of the first and second journeys. Moreover, Antioch is important to the New Testament narrative because there believers were first called Christians (Acts 11:26). It is no wonder that Paul selected that center as a base of operations, because Antioch admirably fitted into his plan for evangelizing large urban centers that might serve as hubs of missionary activity. Antioch was the third city of the Roman Empire, after Rome and Alexandria. Population estimates for the city and its suburbs run as high as eight hundred thousand, but probably a figure of five hundred thousand is more realistic. Antioch was located on the left bank of the Orontes, about twenty miles from the Mediterranean. In that position, it benefited from all the north-south caravan trade; and through its seaport, Seleucia Pieria, flowed the goods and ideas of the Roman world. Moreover, Jews were privileged citizens of the city, and they probably numbered about one-seventh of the total population, making a great religious and economic impact on the area.[25] Many of the Greeks became God-fearers there.

Antioch was founded about 300 B.C. by Seleucus I Nicator in honor of his father and became the most famous of the sixteen Antiochs that he built. Various Seleucid kings added sections to the city, until by the first century A.D. it had four walled quarters. Antioch became a part of the Roman Empire in 64 B.C. but retained its status as a free city. The metropolis was laid out in imitation of Alexandria, with two great covered colonnaded streets intersecting at the center, making it possible to walk the entire length of the city sheltered from sun and rain. From time to time other colonnaded streets were added. Antiochenes spared no efforts to beautify their city. Parks and fountains abounded; public buildings were lovely to look upon. In fact, Antioch was known throughout the Roman world for its splendor.

But it was known for its moral corruption, too. Four to five miles from the city lay the beautiful groves of Daphne, about ten miles in circumference. The stately cyprus trees, lovely gardens and villas, and scenic waterfalls hardly betrayed the evils practiced in the name of religion at the sanctuary of Apollo there. Indeed, "Daphnic morals" permeated the whole moral fiber of the populace, and the city easily ranked with Corinth in its reputation for evil. We may well suspect that the iniquity of Antioch became full, as did the iniquity of the Amorites (see chapter 2). The hand of God fell upon the city in the form of a very destructive earthquake in 526, and Antioch was burned to the ground by the Persian King Chosroes in 540. The modern city of Antakya, with its population of some 100 thousand, occupies only a part of the ancient site, a fact that has been a boon to the excavators who have worked there. The population was only about one-third its present size when excavations were conducted there earlier in the century.

Excavations were carried on at Antioch from 1932 to 1939 by Princeton University, with the cooperation of the Baltimore Museum of Art, the Worcester Art Museum, and the National Museum of France, under the general direction of Richard Stillwell. The main features of the city plan were recovered, and the near equivalent has

---

25. Bruce M. Metzger, "Antioch-on-the-Orontes," *The Biblical Archaeologist*, December 1948, p. 81.

been accomplished for Daphne and Seleucia. The acropolis of the city was discovered on Mount Stauris; the location of the two principal colonnaded streets was plotted; and the circus, probably erected originally in the first century, was found and excavated. Villas, aqueducts, and baths in abundance were found at Antioch and her two suburbs. Portions of the city wall survive on the hill slopes, some as much as forty feet high and eleven feet thick. Several churches were uncovered; one, St. Peter's Church, is alleged to date to the first century; no other first-century Christian remains were discovered. Probably most amazing of all the finds at Antioch were the abundant and well-executed mosaics, dating from the first to the sixth centuries. Although none of them have any particular bearing on the New Testament, they have served to enrich our knowledge of ancient culture.

By means of archaeological and historical sources, we are now able to picture with considerable detail Antioch-on-the-Orontes as Paul knew it—with all of its beauty, wealth, culture, and immorality. As was true of other major urban centers, the gospel was victorious there, and Antioch became a great center of Christian learning and evangelism. More than thirty church synods were held there during the early centuries of the Christian era.

Ephesus—Worshiper of Diana

Visited by Paul on his second missionary journey, Ephesus gained extended attention on his third journey, when he ministered there about three years (Acts 20:31). Although Pergamum was the legal capital of the Roman province of Asia during the first century A.D., Ephesus was for all practical purposes the real capital of the province. Religiously, it served as a great center for the worship of Diana, or Artemis; during the Artemision (the sacred month corresponding to parts of our March and April) pilgrims came to the metropolis from all parts of the province. Politically, it was the administrative seat; the governor had his palace there. Commercially, her position was ideal. Ephesus was situated on the Cayster River, which served as a channel to the Mediterranean, about four miles away. While her sheltered harbor caused some maintenance problems, it provided excellent protection for shipping. She sat astride the highway into the interior of Asia Minor and thus, between sea and land routes, handled a tremendous amount of east-west trade; moreover, she was a major center on the north-south road through Asia.

Ephesus was gradually deserted after about 1350, and it slumbered under the dust of the centuries until brought to light by archaeologists during the latter part of the nineteenth century. Now it is one of the most exciting archaeological triumphs of the Mediterranean world. The English architect J. T. Wood began systematic excavation at the site in 1863; he continued his work until 1874. In 1896 Otto Benndorf and Rudolf Heberdey, representing the Austrian Archaeological Institute, began an extended excavation at the site; and D. G. Hogarth excavated for the British Museum there in 1904-1905. Austrian archaeologists continue to work annually at Ephesus.

Wood's chief object of search at Ephesus was the temple of Diana, but he was destined to labor six years before finding it—about a mile from the city wall. After he did locate this seventh wonder of the ancient world, it took him five more years to excavate it. The raised temple platform measured 239 feet in width and 418 feet in length; the building itself was 180 feet wide and 377 feet long. Its roof was supported by 117 columns six feet in diameter and sixty feet high. Many of them were sculptured around the base with life-size figures. Wood learned that white, blue, red, and yellow marble had been employed in the various parts of the temple. In the ruins he also found several splendidly executed statues of Greco-Roman gods. A most amazing discovery at the site of the temple was made by Hogarth in 1904. While working around the structure that Wood had identified as the great altar, he found it to be hollow. Upon breaking it open, he brought to light a great array of jewelry, coins, and objets d'art. That horde of treasure apparently constituted a foundation deposit—a sort of cornerstone that must have been laid when the temple was begun during the fourth century B.C.

As already mentioned, the Ephesus of Paul's day has been extensively excavated. It is to the Austrians that we owe credit for most of the excavation of the city itself. The city wall, measuring approximately five miles in length, enclosed an area of over a thousand acres. Most imposing of the structures within the city was the great theater, interesting to the New Testament student as the scene of a tumult caused by Paul's ministry. Perched on the western slope of Mount Pion, the theater held an estimated twenty-five thousand persons. In front of the theater was a small square, on one side of which stood a great double-arched gate leading into the Arkadiane. This marble-paved thoroughfare led to the harbor, almost half a mile away. There it passed through a magnificent harbor gate. The street itself was thirty-six feet wide and was bordered on either side by a colonnade, behind which shops were located.

From the south side of the theater plaza ran the main street of the city. After passing the great 360-foot square Hellenistic *agora* or marketplace, the marble street turned to the southeast. On its way to the Magnesian Gate it passed some expensive villas on the right and the Odeion (music hall or small theater) and town hall on the left. Sprawling over a considerable area near the Magnesian Gate was the Roman agora, now excavated.

While Paul was in Ephesus, his main opposition came from Demetrius, a silversmith who made silver miniatures of the temple of Diana, probably for the pilgrim trade (Acts 19:24). To date none of those has been unearthed; nor is such a discovery very likely. In time of war, objects made of valuable metals are plundered first from a city. Moreover, many of them may have been melted down as their owners became Christian. It should be noted, however, that miniature marble and terra cotta shrines have been found in the ruins.

In spite of the fierce antagonism Paul met in his ministry at Ephesus, the gospel triumphed. After the martyrdom of Paul and the destruction of Jerusalem, the beloved apostle John became leader of the church there. Archaeologists found the sixth-century church of St. John north of the temple of Diana and located in it the traditional tomb of the apostle. In the days of John the population of Ephesus reached perhaps 500,000. Later centuries saw the city take on increasing significance as a center of church power and influence. Here was held the famous Council of Ephesus in 431 to deal with theological controversies over the nature of the person of Christ. The great church of St. Mary, where that council was held, has also been completely uncovered by archaeological effort. It stood to the northwest of the theater near the harbor of Ephesus.

Corinth—A Center for European Evangelization

When Paul invaded the great commercial center of Corinth in A.D.

50 or 51, he preached not to the rival of Athens and Sparta during the classical age but to a new city less than a hundred years old. Ancient Corinth had been destroyed by the Romans in 146 B.C. as a punishment for continued insurrection. So important was the site from a commercial standpoint, however, that Julius Caesar repopulated it in 44 B.C. The population grew so rapidly that when Paul ministered there for eighteen months (Acts 18:11) during his second missionary journey, he had a large parish, probably considerably in excess of one hundred thousand persons. Greeks, Jews, and Orientals mixed with Roman military colonists in this city, which became the Roman province of Achaia.

The importance of Corinth lay in her geographical position. Located a mile and a half south of the Isthmus of Corinth, she commanded that four-mile-wide neck of land, as well as its eastern port of Cenchrea (Acts 18:18) and its western port of Lechaeum. In New Testament as well as classical times, a tremendous amount of shipping passed through Greek waters, and the voyage around the southern tip of Greece was not only long but extremely dangerous. Therefore, it became customary to transport goods across the Isthmus of Corinth. Smaller ships were pulled across the isthmus on a tramway; larger ones were unloaded and their cargoes reloaded on the other side. Short stretches of that tramway can still be seen. Since the opening of the Corinth Canal in 1893, that laborious means of shipping has become unnecessary.

The commercial importance of Corinth demonstrates the possibilities of an apostolic ministry there. Not only was the population large and heterogeneous, but it was moving. Sailors and businessmen from all parts of the empire disembarked at her ports. When won for the gospel, they would become missionaries in their home communities and wherever else their business took them. Perhaps here is in part an explanation for the origin of the church at Rome to which Paul addressed an epistle a few years later. Possibly it solves the problem of how the apostle knew so many people in the capital, where he had never been (see Romans 16).

It was only during the last century that Old Corinth was completely abandoned after destruction by an earthquake, though of course the city endured many partial destructions during previous centuries. In 1896 the American School of Classical Studies began excavation there under the general direction of Dr. R. B. Richardson and continued for a total of thirty seasons. The site has been extensively cleared, at least in the central area around the agora.

Dominating the city on the southwest was the Acro-Corinth, a rocky promontory almost two thousand feet high. Atop that stood the temple of Aphrodite, where corrupt religious orgies took place. There a thousand priestesses were employed in religious prostitution, and from that source (along with the fact that much of the population was transient and therefore cut off from the inhibitions of a settled society) arose a general corruption of the morals of the city. Against that Paul fought in 1 Corinthians, where he emphasized the sacredness of the body.

In the center of Corinth, surrounded by remains of residences, the excavators found the great agora, or marketplace, of the city. It measured about six hundred feet east to west and about three hundred north to south. It was divided by a row of commercial buildings that separated the lower northern portion of the agora from the higher southern level. Stairways connected the two levels. In the middle of this row of buildings stood the great *rostra*, or *bema*, which served as a speaker's stand for public addresses and a judgment seat for magistrates. Originally covered with ornately carved marble, that structure even in its poorly preserved condition still gives evidence of former magnificence. Officials reached the bema from the higher southern level, and those who appeared to present their case or to be judged stood on the lower northern level. The bema is of particular interest to the New Testament student because Paul stood before it when Gallio was proconsul of Achaia.

At the northeast corner of the agora was located the famous Peirene Fountain, one of the best-known fountains of antiquity. It furnished much of the water supply of the city. Shops lined the northwest and western sides of the agora; and along the southern side ran a Doric colonnade over 500 feet in length, behind which were situated thirty-three small rooms used as meat markets or wine shops. In the rear of each was another small room with a well connected to the Peirene Fountain. Into those wells wine and meat were lowered for refrigeration. In one of the shops appeared an inscription revealing that it was a meat or fish market. In the inscription, *macellum* was employed—the very word translated *shambles* in 1 Corinthians 10:25. Perhaps what Paul was trying to tell his readers, then, was to ask no questions about meats sold in the shops on the southern side of the city. It was not the responsibility of customers to determine the origin of a merchant's wares.

The road from the port of Cenchrea led into the eastern side of the agora, and the road to Lechaeum joined it at the northeast corner. The hard limestone blocks of that thoroughfare are still in good condition. An interesting find excavated near the Lechaeum Road was a block bearing the inscription, "Synagogue of the Hebrews." It is thought to be a lintel from the Jewish synagogue of Corinth, and it is possible that the synagogue in which Paul preached stood there. At the east end of the agora stood the Julian basilica, a structure where many of the court cases of litigious Corinthian Christians may have been heard (1 Corinthians 6:1-7).

Volumes could be filled with a description of the details of the excavations at Corinth. We could tell of the great theater, the temple of Apollo, the Glauke Fountain, temples lining the approaches to the Acro-Corinth, public buildings, statuary, the *odeion* (music hall), private dwellings, and the thousands of pieces of pottery and other small objects, as well as the many inscriptions. But perhaps the buildings most important for New Testament illumination have been mentioned.

One more inscription might be noted, however. One of the paving blocks still in place near the theater bears an inscription saying that it was laid at the expense of Erastus, chamberlain of the city. Perhaps this was the same Corinthian Erastus known to Paul (Acts 19:22; Romans 16:23).

Such, then, was the metropolis to which Paul preached—in synagogue, agora, and home of Justus. The excavations demonstrate that it was a city geared to business pursuits. Perhaps it was almost too busy to listen to the message of God. Yet Paul had a successful ministry there, and a fairly large church was established—to be plagued during succeeding decades by moral laxity and the other sins of a pagan atmosphere.

10

Ancient Libraries and the Bible

The "libraries" discussed in this chapter were not libraries in the modern sense of the term—collections where scholars or the general public might go to do research or to read for amusement, or from which books might be checked out. But they were libraries in the sense of being archives kept for reference by officials of state or certain private persons. And at least the royal library of Assyria was designed to be an extensive collection of literature amassed for future reference.

Fortunately, archaeologists have uncovered many collections of ancient texts. No doubt many other libraries await discovery, but probably some of the greatest ones were destroyed or have deteriorated and disappeared. In the latter category is the court archive of Persia at Achmetha (Ecbatana, Ezra 6:2) and the Babylonian and Persian archive at Babylon (Ezra 6:1). The mention of a scroll in Ezra 6:2 leads to the belief that some of those records disintegrated in the climate to which they were subjected; or perhaps they were destroyed when Alexander the Great came through in 331 B.C. or during later administrations.

Numerous ancient Near Eastern libraries have made a great impact on biblical studies. A few of the more important are the library of Ashurbanipal at Nineveh, other great Mesopotamian collections at Nuzi and Mari, the Hittite archives at Boghaz-Koi, the valuable Syrian repositories at Ugarit and Ebla, and the highly touted library of Qumran.[1]

Mesopotamian Collections

Nineveh. In any discussion of libraries of the ancient Near East, pride of place must go to the library of King Ashurbanipal of Assyria (668-633 B.C.), the Osnappar of the Old Testament (Ezra 4:10). It was probably the first systematically collected library in the ancient Near East, and it was found first. Though a library of sorts had been in existence at the Temple of Nabu at Nineveh for some fifty years, it was Ashurbanipal who sent scribes all over Assyria and Babylonia to copy and translate Sumerian, Akkadian, Babylonian, and Assyrian texts containing historical, scientific, and religious literature, official and business documents, and private communications "as precious possessions of my royalty."

The original size of the Assyrian imperial library is impossible to determine, but more than twenty-five thousand clay tablets from it (representing about then thousand texts) found their way to the British Museum in London. Nearly all of these came as a result of Hormuzd Rassam's excavations at Nineveh, 1852 to 1853. But George Smith of the museum staff discovered some additional tablets in 1872.

This horde of literature is significant, first, because it provides abundant material for the study of Assyrian and the establishment of its grammar and the meaning of words. Second, many tablets contain dated references and thus help to refine the chronology of Mesopotamia. Third, the variety of material representing many aspects of life contributes to an understanding of the context in which the biblical narrative developed. Last, there were in the library some parallels to the Old Testament. For example, a poem of a righteous sufferer portrays a kind of Babylonian Job. A creation account (the *Enuma Elish*) and a flood account (the *Gilgamesh Epic*) also have numerous similarities to the biblical record, although they also contain many marked differences. Alexander Heidel of the University of Chicago dealt with the problem of the relationship of these texts to Scripture in *The*

---

1. Brief introductions to decipherment of some of the languages involved in these libraries may be found in Howard F. Vos, *Archaeology in Bible Lands* (Chicago: Moody, 1977), pp. 30-39; and Cyrus H. Gordon, *Forgotten Scripts*, rev. ed. (New York: Basic Books, 1982).

Babylonian Genesis and *The Gilgamesh Epic* and concluded that neither the biblical nor the Babylonian accounts borrowed from the other but that similarities derived from the fact that both arose from the same general context or source.

Nuzi. The archives from Nuzi, or Nuzu, in northeastern Iraq are of an entirely different character from those of Nineveh. The some twenty thousand cuneiform tablets consist of social documents and letters found in large private houses excavated at the site. Though Nuzi had a long history, its era most significant for biblical study was the Hurrian period (about 1500 B.C.), to which the tablets date.

The private archives reveal the thinking and affairs of leading citizens of the time and provide interesting parallels to patriarchal customs. At Nuzi there is evidence of the sale of the birthright (cf. Esau), use of the oral blessing (cf. Isaac, Jacob), practice of the wife's giving a slave girl to her husband to bear children (cf. Sarah, Leah, Rachel), adoption of an heir (cf. Abraham and Eliezer), and more. Thus it is possible to observe those customs in action in the same general area of northern Mesopotamia where Abraham lived for a while and where some of his relatives continued to live.

Excavations at Nuzi were conducted between 1925 and 1931 by the American Schools of Oriental Research, in cooperation with the Iraq Museum, Harvard, and the University of Pennsylvania Museum. Edward Chiera, Robert H. Pfeiffer, and R. F. S. Starr directed the several seasons of work there.

Mari. Mari, located in the middle Euphrates region just north of the present Syria-Iraq border, is sometimes classified as a Syrian city. André Parrot of the Louvre excavated there from 1933 to 1939 and from 1951 to 1956. Other French teams have been working there since. Though the ziggurat and the temples of Mari are very interesting, the palace and its archives are especially relevant to the present study. The palace covered about eight acres and consisted of three hundred rooms and corridors arranged around open courts. The royal archives, containing about twenty-five thousand clay tablets, were written mostly in Akkadian, but some texts were in Hurrian. To date, about one-fifth of them have been published. The city had a long history, but the period most significant for present purposes was the one dating about 1700 B.C., when Hammurabi conquered and leveled the site.

Many of the documents represent diplomatic correspondence between King Zimri-Lim of Mari and Hammurabi and thus help to establish the chronology of Mesopotamia during the second millennium B.C. They also contain names equivalent to those mentioned in Genesis 11:16, 23, 24, 27 (e.g., Peleg, Serug, Nahor), showing that they were good historical names. Many linguistic expressions and cultural concepts appearing in the Old Testament are also found in the Mari texts. For example, the "judge" in Mari fulfilled a primarily administrative function rather than a judicial one, as was true of the Old Testament judges. Moreover, the Mari tablets mention customs reflected in the patriarchal narrative and throw light on the tribal organization and traditions of Syria in patriarchal times.

Hittite Archives

As late as the beginning of the twentieth century critics were asserting that the Hittites did not exist and that biblical writers therefore were in error in referring to them. Then Hugo Winckler launched a German Oriental Society dig at Bogazköy (now officially Bogazkale), about 125 miles east of Ankara by modern road. The large site of more than four hundred acres proved to be the capital of the Hittite Empire, and within a year Winckler uncovered a large Hittite royal archive of about ten thousand clay tablets in the citadel area. Kurt Bittel, also excavating for the German Oriental Society, found another three thousand tablets in the citadel area during the seasons of 1931 to 1933. In 1937 he found another smaller royal cache. The texts make possible a scientific study of Hittite language, provide the means for constructing a history of the Hittites, contribute to a clearer understanding of Near Eastern chronology, and confirm the fact that biblical writers were not in error in referring to the Hittites.

Syrian Repositories

Ugarit. Ancient Ugarit (modern Ras Shamra) stood at a crossroads of ancient civilization. Located on the Syrian coast twenty-five miles south of the mouth of the Orontes River and opposite the island of Cyprus, it dominated the trade between the mainland and that copper-rich island. Though enjoying a long history, Ugarit was at her height of power during the fifteenth and fourteenth centuries B.C. Thus the large collections of tablets that Claude F. A. Schaeffer of the Strasbourg Museum found there beginning in 1929 date to the days of Moses and the founding of the Hebrew theocratic state.

During his very first season, Schaeffer found the temple library near the temple of Dagon, and subsequently he uncovered the state archives in the sprawling stone palace (covering 10,000 square yards). The palace archives were organized systematically in three divisions: texts bearing on fiscal affairs of the provinces (located by the main western entrance), records concerning financial matters of the city (in the eastern archive), and diplomatic correspondence (in the southern archive).

The total collection is in seven languages, written in five scripts. Egyptian, Sumerian, Akkadian, Hurrian, and Hittite texts are useful for understanding the history of the Near East and provide contextual information for Old Testament studies. But of special interest was the large number of materials written in a previously unknown Canaanite alphabetic script now called Ugaritic. Closely related to biblical Hebrew, it provides a knowledge of that language at the time of Moses. It has enabled many previously unknown words in the Old Testament to be identified and the meaning of others made clear. Now scholars can also know Canaanite religion through its own literature, and as a result of a greater knowledge of its depravity, appreciate more fully why the Old Testament so severely condemned it.

Though Ugaritic (Canaanite) religion was terribly depraved, there were numerous institutional similarities between it and the Hebrew religion. For instance, both made "peace offerings" and "burnt offerings" and used comparable sacrificial animals in the process. But while technical terms used by the two systems of worship may have been similar, meanings poured into those terms were in striking contrast. Canaanite mythology and Israelite theology were poles apart, and there is nothing disquieting about the similarities. In fact, the existence of such a highly developed religious and legal system contemporary with Moses is reassuring, for critics used to say that it was impossible for anything so highly developed as the Mosaic system to have arisen so early in Near Eastern history. Now it is no longer tenable to hold that Mosaic religious institutions had to come late in Hebrew history and that Moses could not have been involved with their establishment.

Mardikh-Ebla.[2] University of Rome excavations under the direction of Paolo Matthiae began inauspiciously at Tell Mardikh in 1964 and continued without significant discovery until 1968. In that year a statue of the king of the ancient site came to light. Its dedicatory inscription identified the place as Ebla, an important city-state of northern Syria that had clashed repeatedly with the kingdom of Akkad and was finally destroyed by it about 2200 B.C. As a matter of fact, Ebla, located about thirty-five miles southeast of modern Aleppo, had controlled an empire that extended south to the Sinai, west to Cyprus, east to the highlands of Mesopotamia, and north into the eastern part of Asia Minor. Reportedly, the city with its suburbs had a population of 260,000 at its height.

The 1968 discovery pumped new life into the Mardikh expedition, but the really significant finds were not destined to come for several more years. In 1974 forty-two tablets were discovered; during the following year about fifteen thousand tablets were unearthed; and in 1976 an additional five thousand were uncovered. The Ebla archives were located in an administration building on the western slope of the 140-acre mound. Apparently the structure served as a reception hall for foreign commercial delegations, and there customs duties were imposed.

The texts date to a century or two before 2200 B.C. About 80 percent of them were written in Sumerian and the rest in a hitherto unknown language that Pettinato classified as "Paleo-Canaanite," with affinities to Phoenician and Hebrew and, to a lesser degree, to Ugaritic. Fortunately the ancient scribes produced bilingual texts in Sumerian and "Eblaite," so decipherment could proceed with a high degree of facility.

To date, Eblaite decipherment is in its infancy, but a considerable amount is already known. First, categories of texts are clearly evident. Some are economic in character, dealing with international trade and local administration. Others are literary, containing religious myths, hymns to the gods, and proverbs. A third group deals with legal and political affairs, such as ordinances, edicts, and legal arrangements. A

---

2. In addition to numerous articles on Ebla, three full-length books have been published: Chaim Bermant and Michael Weitzman, *Ebla* (New York: Times Books, 1979); Paolo Matthiae, *Ebla—An Empire Rediscovered* (Garden City, N.Y.: Doubleday, 1981); Giovanni Pettinato, *The Archives of Ebla* (Garden City, N.Y.: Doubleday, 1981).

few are linguistic in character and were designed for teaching Sumerian and/or Eblaite. Closely related in function were tablets that must have served as textbooks in the schools: list of animals, birds, fish, and places.

Second, the tablets evidently have great significance for biblical study and give promise of illuminating the patriarchal and prepatriarchal eras of Genesis. They mention many cities of the Old Testament, including Hazor, Lachish, Megiddo, Gaza, Joppa, Urusalima, (probably the oldest reference to Jerusalem), Haran, and the Cities of the Plain (Genesis 18-19): Sodom, Gomorrah, and Zoar. They record many names that occur in the Old Testament, for example, David, Esau, Saul, Micah, and patriarchal kinds of names such as *Ab-ra-mu* (Abraham). While none of these Eblaite names may have any connection with biblical personalities (for all this literature dates centuries before), at least they show that biblical names are good historical names and need not be taken as symbolic or as inventions of biblical writers, as frequently has been alleged. Since more than 95 percent of the Eblaite texts remains untranslated and most of the site remains unexcavated, no one can predict what new revelations may yet come from northern Syria.

Dead Sea Scrolls

The Qumran library was quite different in content and significance from those mentioned above. To a large degree it was a collection of biblical manuscripts produced by or at least owned by the ascetic community that lived at Qumran, about a mile from the western shore of the Dead Sea and seven and one-half miles south of Jericho. The manuscripts were produced in scroll form on animal skins and were hidden in clay jars in caves near the Qumran community.

The first discoveries of scrolls in the Qumran region occurred in 1947, and they appeared on the antiquities market a few months later, during the partition of Palestine and struggles related to the birth of Israel. Conditions in the area prevented a concerted exploration of caves there for a couple of years. Then, between 1949 and 1956, some 270 caves were scoured by archaeologists and bedouins. Manuscript finds turned up in a total of eleven caves.

When assembled, the contents of Cave 1 included a complete text of Isaiah dating to the second century B.C., a partial Isaiah, a Habakkuk commentary (including two chapters of Habakkuk), *The Manual of Discipline* (rules for members of the religious community who lived nearby), *Thanksgiving Hymns*, a *Genesis Apocryphon* (apocryphal accounts of some of the patriarchs), and *Wars of the Sons of Light Against the Sons of Darkness* (an account of real or spiritual war between some of the Hebrew tribes and tribes east of the Jordan). Excavations of Cave 2 turned up about one hundred fragments of eight biblical books. In Cave 3 excavations produced a curious copper scroll about twelve inches high, with directions to more than sixty sites containing hidden treasure; to date none of that treasure has been found. Cave 4 provided some forty thousand fragments of an unknown number of manuscripts, about four hundred of which have been identified. About one hundred were biblical scrolls and represented all the Old Testament books except Esther. A fragment of Samuel, dating to the third century B.C., is thought to be the oldest known piece of biblical Hebrew. Caves 5 through 10 had a wide variety of scroll fragments. Prize pieces from Cave 11 included a Psalms scroll with forty-one biblical psalms and a large part of Leviticus.

The significance of the Qumran library has been summarized at the end of chapter 6, but a brief statement is in order here. These materials, dating from the third century B.C. to the second century A.D., push back the history of the Old Testament text by well over a thousand years. Their general support of the text that has been in circulation all along helps to demonstrate what might be termed a miracle of the transmission of the Old Testament text. Moreover, many passages in the Old Testament can be more clearly understood now because this body of formal and informal literature throws much light on the meanings of individual words often not clearly comprehended from their Old Testament usage.

11

The Apologetic Value
of Bible Archaeology

Two facts have been evident in the development of this brief study of Bible archaeology: (1) archaeology helps to place the Bible, an oriental book, in its Near Eastern setting and thereby to improve the ability of a Westerner to understand it; (2) this science provides much material that serves to confirm the Scripture. Our interest in this chapter centers on the second truth.

Ample is the testimony to the apologetic value of archaeology, even on the part of liberals. The late William F. Albright of Johns Hopkins said, "There can be no doubt that archaeology has confirmed the substantial historicity of Old Testament tradition."[1] Millar Burrows, formerly of Yale, attested: "On the whole, however, archaeological work has unquestionably strengthened confidence in the reliability of the Scriptural record. More than one archaeologist has found his respect for the Bible increased by the experience of excavation in Palestine."[2] He continued, "Archaeology has in many cases refuted the views of modern critics. It has shown in a number of instances that these views rest on false assumptions and unreal, artificial schemes of historical development. This is a real contribution, and not to be

---

1. William F. Albright, *Archaeology and the Religion of Israel*, 4th ed. (Baltimore: Johns Hopkins, 1956), p. 176.
2. Millar Burrows, *What Mean These Stones?* (New York: Meridian, 1957), p. 1.

minimized."[3] Sir Frederic Kenyon, formerly director of the British Museum, commented:

> It is therefore legitimate to say that, in respect of that part of the Old Testament against which the disintegrating criticism of the last half of the nineteenth century was chiefly directed, the evidence of archaeology has been to re-establish its authority, and likewise to augment its value by rendering it more intelligible through a fuller knowledge of its background and setting. Archaeology has not yet said its last word; but the results already achieved confirm what faith would suggest, that the Bible can do nothing but gain from an increase of knowledge.[4]

We are not to be misled, however, into thinking that liberals have been completely taken aback by recent discoveries in the Middle East. A further statement by Millar Burrows should sufficiently make that clear: "It is quite untrue to say that all the theories of the critics have been overthrown by archaeological discoveries. It is even more untrue to say that the fundamental attitudes and methods of modern scientific criticism have been refuted."[5]

The conservative must keep in mind that while the liberal critic may acknowledge the veracity of certain historical features of Scripture as a result of archaeological investigation, he does not like to admit that this has any bearing on the supernatural element. An illustration of this fact is seen in McCown's attitude toward the biblical narrative of the fall of Jericho. After discussing the results of the excavations at the site he said, "The general dependability of the nonmiraculous features in the record is rendered probable."[6] In other words, he might be willing to accept the account of what happened, but he prefers to believe that the author of Joshua was mistaken as to the reason events transpired as they did (i.e., divine intervention).

Burrows commented further on this matter,

> Much of what is said in the Bible, and that by far the most important part, cannot be tested by archeological evidence. That God is One, that he is Maker of heaven and earth, that man is made in his image, that Christ is the Incarnate Word of God, that by following him man finds eternal life, that the way to abundant life is the way of self-dedication

---

3. Ibid., pp. 291-92.
4. Sir Frederic Kenyon, *The Bible and Archaeology* (New York: Harper, 1940), p. 279.
5. Burrows, p. 292.
6. C. C. McCown, *The Ladder of Progress in Palestine* (New York: Harper, 1943), p. 81.

and love—such teachings are entirely outside the sphere in which archeology or any science can have anything to say. Any attempt to demonstrate the truth of the Bible as revelation by an appeal to archeology necessarily proceeds on the false assumption that truth of one kind and truth of another kind must go together. In other words, it is taken for granted that if the historical record is accurate, the spiritual teaching also is reliable. . . . Religious truth is one thing; historical fact is another. Neither necessarily presupposes or accompanies the other.[7]

We must concede to Burrows that evangelicals have, perhaps, overemphasized the connection between the historical and theological elements of Sacred Writ and without question often have tried to prove too much; but the two elements do go together and must not be entirely divorced. Since it has been a trick of opponents of the gospel to cast doubt on the theological message of the Bible by attacking its historical and scientific references, may we not conclude that the spiritual message is strengthened whenever archaeology demonstrates the veracity of the context of a theological dictum?

The last two quotations should help us to realize that an archaeological apologetic may not be of great value when used on men educated in the liberal line of thought. In fact, the apologetic approach never has been very successful in winning avowed opponents of the truth. None of the Roman emperors was brought within the fold by the impassioned apologies addressed to them by the leaders of the early church. The two theological camps of the twentieth century—liberal and conservative—follow antithetical sets of postulates: the one nonsupernatural and the other supernatural. An apologetic can bring a liberal to agreement only on historical features. It cannot cause him to reverse himself on the issue of the supernatural. We do not mean to say, however, that such men are beyond the reach of the gospel; certainly the Holy Spirit can woo them to the Son, even though all of our academic approaches may fail.

But there is a class of non-Christians with whom one may use an archaeological apologetic effectively. Those are individuals who are close to salvation but find that certain intellectual difficulties pose hurdles too great for them to leap. In that case, a few solutions may be offered from the field of archaeology in order to dispel the doubts, and

7. Burrows, pp. 3-4.

the person might ultimately be brought to know the Lord through a witness begun in that way.

The archaeological apologetic performs its greatest ministry in the life of the believer, however. It helps him to stand true to the faith in the classroom where the attacks on all he holds dear are very great. It adds external factual support for his faith as doubts arise within. It strengthens him in his activity in the world at large as he faces the skeptical barbs of the literature he reads and the people with whom he comes in contact. If the knowledge of archaeology can do all that for the Christian, it behooves him to study it assiduously in order that it may become a more effective weapon in his hand for dealing with personal doubts and opposition and in engaging more effectively in presenting the message of the gospel.

Books for Further Study

It is at the same time fortunate and disconcerting that there are now so many books available in the field of Bible archaeology and related studies. Where is one to begin? What books are most useful or easiest to get? Which are theologically sound? In a sense the following suggestions try to answer all those questions. Specialized, technical, and out-of-print books are omitted.

For a Beginning

One of the most useful general books is J. A. Thompson's *The Bible and Archaeology* (Grand Rapids: Eerdmans, 1962). It has sections on Old Testament archaeology, the intertestamental background, and New Testament archaeology. Another work that covers the whole field but has some objectionable features from a theological standpoint is G. Ernest Wright's *Biblical Archaeology*, rev. ed. (Philadelphia: Westminster, 1963). In the same category but more objective is Jack Finegan's excellent *Light from the Ancient Past*, 2d ed. (Princeton: Princeton U., 1959). An extremely useful reference book is *The Biblical World*, edited by Charles Pfeiffer (Grand Rapids: Baker, 1966). A dictionary of biblical archaeology, it has articles on excavations at biblical sites and subjects related to biblical archaeology. A new dictionary that admirably covers the entire field is *The New International*

113

Dictionary of Biblical Archaeology, ed. E. M. Blaiklock and R. K. Harrison (Grand Rapids: Zondervan, 1983). A recent general work on the whole field of biblical archaeology is Howard F. Vos, *Archaeology in Bible Lands* (Chicago: Moody, 1977). This book deals with archaeological technique, history of excavation, and discoveries related to the text of the Bible; and it provides brief statements on all Bible sites excavated to date. Another of the newer works is Keith Schoville's *Biblical Archaeology in Focus* (Grand Rapids: Baker, 1978). It deals individually with numerous excavated sites in the Near East as well as various introductory topics.

On Old Testament Archaeology

Old favorites in the field of Old Testament archaeology are Ira M. Price and others, *The Monuments and the Old Testament* (Philadelphia: Judson, 1958), and Merrill F. Unger's *Archaeology and the Old Testament* (Grand Rapids: Zondervan, 1954). A more recent, briefer treatment is R. K. Harrison's *Archaeology of the Old Testament* (London: English Universities Press, 1963).

Excavations at numerous Old Testament sites are discussed by a variety of specialists in *Archaeology and Old Testament Study*, edited by D. Winton Thomas (Oxford: Clarendon, 1967). James B. Pritchard has rendered an invaluable service in editing two basic reference works on Old Testament archaeology. The first is *Ancient Near Eastern Texts Relating to the Old Testament*, 2d ed. (Princeton: Princeton U., 1955), and the second is *Ancient Near East in Pictures Relating to the Old Testament*, 2d ed. (Princeton: Princeton U., 1969).

On New Testament Archaeology

Fortunately we are beginning to witness the production of materials on New Testament archaeology. For too long people have been led to believe that archaeology was concerned only with the Old Testament.

Merrill F. Unger published his *Archaeology and the New Testament* in 1962 (Grand Rapids: Zondervan). It was followed two years later by R. K. Harrison's *Archaeology of the New Testament* (London: English Universities Press). Then Jack Finegan produced his *Archeology of the New Testament* (Princeton: Princeton U., 1969), which centered largely on the life of Christ. Now Jack Finegan has finished the second part of *The Archeology of the New Testament: The Mediterranean World of the Early Christian Apostles* (Boulder, Colo.: Westview, 1982). E. M. Blaiklock wrote a more general work entitled *The Archaeology of the New Testament* (Grand Rapids: Zondervan, 1970). Edwin Yamauchi has provided a useful study of some of the cities of Paul, *The Archaeology of New Testament Cities in Western Asia Minor* (Grand Rapids: Baker, 1980).

If we are not to neglect classical archaeology as it bears on the New Testament, we should mention Paul MacKendrick's companion volumes, *The Mute Stones Speak* (New York: St. Martin's, 1960), which deals with Italy, and *The Greek Stones Speak* (New York: St. Martin's, 1962), which tells the story of archaeology in Greece, adjacent islands, and Greco-Roman sites in Turkey (e.g., Ephesus).

Of Special Interest

Of course special attention centers on Palestine as a field for archaeological endeavor. Two books with well-established reputations in this area are William F. Albright's *The Archaeology of Palestine*, rev. ed. (Harmondsworth, Middlesex: Pelican Books, 1960) and Kathleen Kenyon's *Archaeology in the Holy Land*, rev. ed. (New York: Norton, 1979). A work providing details on excavations at Palestinian sites is *Encyclopedia of Archaeological Excavations in the Holy Land*, edited by Michael Avi-Yonah and Ephraim Stern (Englewood Cliffs, N.J.: Prentice-Hall, vol. 1, 1975; vol. 2, 1976; vol. 3, 1977; vol. 4, 1978).

Another field of special interest is the Dead Sea Scrolls. Much has been written on the subject, but some of the best books are out of print. A most useful book from a factual and theological standpoint is fortunately in paper edition: Charles F. Pfeiffer, *The Dead Sea Scrolls and the Bible* (Grand Rapids: Baker, 1969).

For some decades, the basic nontechnical magazine in the field of biblical archaeology has been *Biblical Archaeologist*, published quarterly by the American Schools of Oriental Research. Although individuals of various theological persuasions write in this publication, its approach is generally factual. Since not all back issues are available, it is good to know that three volumes of *The Biblical Archaeologist Reader* have been published (Garden City, N.Y.: Anchor Books, 1961, 1964,

1970); those paperback editions are collections of some of the best articles of earlier years.

The Biblical Archaeology Review has now taken its place alongside the *Biblical Archaeologist*. Published six times a year, it seeks by popular articles and outstanding graphics to make the past live again.

General Index

Abraham, 19, 21, 23, 79-83
Ahab, 67, 69, 73, 88
Albright, W. F., 15, 33, 57, 80, 109
Alexandrinus, Codex, 46
Amarna, 56
Antioch of Syria, 25, 27, 92-94
Archaeology. *See also* Excavation
  definition of, 13-14
  function of, 14-15, 109-12
Ashurbanipal, 87, 102
Asia Minor, geography of, 26-27
Assyria, 18, 22-23, 66, 73-77, 85-87,
  101-3

Babel, Tower of, 90-91
Babylon, 23, 33, 62-63, 76-77, 89-92,
  101
Babylonia, 23
Bethel, 58-59
British Museum, 32, 102
Burrows, Millar, 49, 109-11

Carbon 14 dating, 43-44
Chronology, 39-43, 80-81
Corinth, 27-28, 96-99
Cyprus, geography of, 27
Cyrus, 62-64, 79
Cyrus Cylinder, 63

Damascus, 23, 25
David, 25, 60-62, 66
Dead Sea, 24
Dead Sea Scrolls, 52, 107-8
Debir, 58, 59
Deissmann, Adolf, 50-51

Ebla Tablets, 106-7
Egypt
  chronology of, 40-41
  geography of, 24-25
Ephesus, 94-96
Esdraelon, 24
Euphrates, 22, 79, 90
Excavation. *See also* Archaeology
  conduct of, 31-38
  technique, 35-37

Exodus
  from Egypt, 55-60, 80
  Pharaoh of, 59-60
Ezion-geber, 32, 66, 70-72

Galilee, Sea of, 23-24
Garstang, John, 56, 69, 84-85
Glueck, Nelson, 57, 70-72
Greece, geography of, 27-28
Gregorian Calendar, 39
Grenfell, B. P., 48
Guy, P. L. O., 67-68

Hammurabi, 23, 81, 89-90
Harvard University, 32, 88, 103
Hazor, 58, 69, 107
Hezekiah, 74-75
Hittite archives, 104
Hort, F. J. A., 47
Hunt, A. S., 48

Iran, geography of, 26
Italy, geography of, 28-29

Jehu, 73
Jericho, 19, 59-60, 83-85
Jerusalem, 28, 60-62, 69, 107
Jezreel, 24
Jonah, 86-87
Jordan River, 24
Josiah, 75-76

Kenyon, Frederic, 46, 49, 53, 110
Kenyon, Kathleen, 36, 60, 62, 84-85
Koldewey, Robert, 90-92

Lachish, 33, 58-59, 107
Layard, A. H., 85

Malta, geography of, 28
Manetho, 41
Mardikh. *See* Ebla Tablets
Mari Tablets, 103
Megiddo, 31, 67-68, 73, 107
Merneptah, 59

Moody Press, a ministry of the Moody Bible Institute, is designed for education, evangelization, and edification. If we may assist you in knowing more about Christ and the Christian life, please write us without obligation: Moody Press, c/o MLM, Chicago, Illinois 60610.